T of

Competition Law

Two week loan

Please return on or before the last date stamped below.
Charges are made for late return.

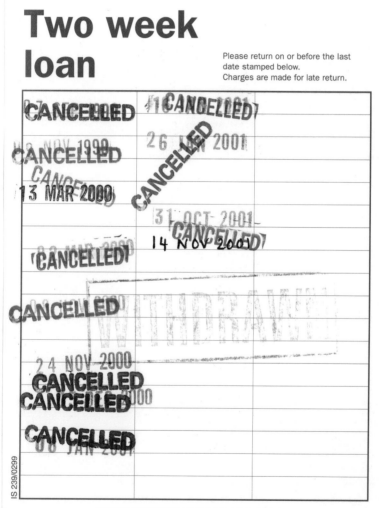

The Europeanisation of United Kingdom Competition Law

EDITED BY

NICHOLAS GREEN
QC, LLM, Ph.D., Barrister

AND

AIDAN ROBERTSON
MA, LLM, Barrister

HART PUBLISHING
OXFORD – PORTLAND OREGON
1999

Hart Publishing
Oxford and Portland, Oregon

Published in North America (US and Canada) by
Hart Publishing c/o
International Specialized Book Services
5804 NE Hassalo Street
Portland, Oregon
97213-3644
USA

Distributed in Netherlands, Belgium and Luxembourg by
Intersentia, Churchillaan 108
B2900 Schoten
Antwepen
Belgium

Distributed in Australia and New Zealand by
Federation Press
John St
Leichhardt
NSW 2000

Hart Publishing is a specialist legal publisher based in
Oxford, England. To order further copies of this book or to
request a list of other publications please write to:

Hart Publishing, 19 Whitehouse Road, Oxford, OX1 4PA
Telephone: +44 (0) 1865 434459 Fax: +44 (0) 1865 794882
email: hartpub@janep.demon.co.uk

British Library Cataloguing in Publication Data
Data Available

ISBN 1 84113-036-2

Typeset by John Saunders Design & Production, Reading
Printed in Great Britain on acid-free paper
by Biddles Ltd, Guildford and King's Lynn

Contents

Preface

The papers in this book were given at a conference organised by the Centre for the Law of the European Union at University College London on 10th September 1998 on the basis of the proposals in the Competition Bill. The Royal Assent was granted to the Competition Act on 9th November 1998 and all the papers have since been cross-referenced to the Act as adopted. The main powers of the Act should be in force on 1st March 2000.

Table of Cases

Table of Legislation

Table of Treaties

1

The Europeanisation of United Kingdom Competition Law

JUDGE CHRISTOPHER BELLAMY

The Competition Act clearly marks a most important evolution in the domestic competition law of the United Kingdom, as Margaret Bloom has explained to us. I do not think it would be appropriate for me to comment in any detail on the provisions of the Bill or how it is likely to be implemented. So I thought I would offer you some reflections of a rather more general, even philosophical, nature, mainly about the possible strengths and weaknesses of a competition policy based in substance on Articles 85 and 86 of the EC Treaty.

My first reflection is historical. I am sure that this Act represents a necessary and probably long overdue modernisation of United Kingdom competition law. But in making that rather unsurprising observation I would myself pay tribute to the now somewhat maligned Restrictive Trade Practices Acts which have been for 42 years the basis of United Kingdom domestic law on restrictive agreements.

You will remember that the Restrictive Trade Practices Act ("RTPA") was originally conceived as a means of decartelising British industry, which had become effectively cartelised in the 1920s and -30s behind the tariff barriers erected after the First World War and during the Great Depression, although much less so than in Germany where the formalised *Kartell* (which of course gives rise to the word "cartel") was the dominant form of industrial organisation from the 1880s right through to 1945.

In 1950s Britain, the weapon used to dismantle the cartels of the 1930s (which incidentally, had also provided a warwinning contribution in the 1940s) was the RTPA, and that was based effectively on three principles. First, the system of registration based on a legal rather than an effects based test. In modern Eurospeak one would say that the principle of legal certainty had prevailed. *La sécurité juridique* was regarded by the legislators as more important than the effects of a particular agreement. Secondly, a public register which was based on what would now be called the principle of transparency, namely, that if people are to make or to be permitted to operate restrictive agreements that should be done in a public way so that everybody knows what is happening, and that there should be no possibility of hidden deals between the industry and the regulators. Not an entirely inappropriate principle. And thirdly, the possibility of justifying an agreement based on the public interest as defined in the various gateways in section 19 of the RTPA, which, when you read them, are not unlike Article 85(3) of the Treaty even though they predate that provision by some 18 months.

So there were strengths, or some strengths, in that legislation in the context of the time. Of course there were no sanctions, or hardly any sanctions, other than to modern eyes the somewhat bizarre possibility of being in contempt of court for making an agreement to the like effect as one condemned by the Restrictive Practices Court. And not until 1968 was there any action for damages for breach of statutory duty, and even then that action was based on failure to register and not on the anticompetitive effect of the agreement concerned.

Thus, it may be contended that the legislation was an honourable effort to address some problems that are at the heart of competition law. One problem in particular is how to combine effective competition with legal certainty. It is interesting to go back to the 1956 debate. It was said in Parliament at the time, we cannot contemplate going down the route of the Sherman Act. The rules are not clear. It is entirely up to judges to decide. You are at risk. You can be sent to prison for playing golf with your friends. Treble damages suits can arrive after a friendly telephone call to a competitor, etc. So the route chosen was a legal route, and it worked in the 1950s and 1960s. Now that was in those rather far off, but possibly more gentlemanly, days, when cartels were in the public domain, run by respectable secretaries and publicly known about.

However, that legislation broke down those cartels and effectively two things happened. The first was that restrictive agreements, in so far as they continued to be made, went underground, and the RTPA was not effective in catching them because it contained no sanctions and because there were no effective powers of investigation. And, secondly, the agreements that were caught by the RTPA were on the whole considered somewhat innocuous, and therefore gave rise to a great deal of administrative effort for very little gain. But the fact remains that whatever the defects of that system, if you go down an effects-based route like the EC route, you throw up other problems because an effects-based system in its pure form is frankly unmanageable. It is totally impractical. If you adopt a wide-ranging test like that adopted by the Court of Justice in *Etablissements Consten SARL and Grundig-Verkaufs-GmbH v. Commission*[1], in the mid1960s, you

---

[1] Cases 56 and 58/64 [1966] ECR 299.

immediately find that to make it workable you have to adopt a whole series of exemptions and exceptions, in order to give back to business the legal certainty that it needs and to reduce the administrative burden on the authorities to within manageable limits.

It is often said that soon after *Consten and Grundig*, the French judiciary in particular, visiting the Court of Justice, said we read your judgment, we see what you say, but we cannot cope with all this. If we are expected to do a market analysis in every case in which somebody raises the illegality or voidness of an agreement being sued on, that is just not practical in terms of time, expense and effort. And that was in fact what happened, although I do not criticise it because it is very hard to find a solution to the problem. What in fact has happened in EC terms is that, at the beginning, a very wide interpretation of Article 85 was adopted and that has formed the basis of a whole series of exempting regulations which you are all familiar with, running through patent licences, distribution agreements, motor vehicles, air and maritime transport, research and development, specialisation, beer, petrol stations and so on and so forth. Exemptions that are extremely well intentioned, but in my experience very seldom fit the particular case that the particular lawyer has on his desk. So if you go down the opposite route from the RTPA you have complications as well. Perhaps one of the tasks in implementing the Competition Act in the United Kingdom, of which I am sure the authorities are well aware, is to try to keep that process of exemption and exception as simple and as comprehensible as possible.

My next reflection is the whole subject of justification, which as I have said is dealt with in the RTPA by the gateway approach. Even in the United States it was realised, if not by the end of 1890 when the Sherman Act was adopted, at least by 1891 or 1892, that, taken literally, it was absurd to declare, in Section 1 of that Act, that any contract in restraint of trade to be illegal. Taken to the extreme, it was a concept that was hardly workable because, as Neale and Goyder point out, at the limit: "[e]very contract between two people, every bargain, is in a sense a restriction of trade because it prevents other deals being done with other traders in the market place and a simple contract may of itself have quite a significant exclusionary effect".

But of course you cannot say that trade itself is a restraint of trade. So the solution adopted in the United States, gradually, is to develop the rule of reason, whereby certain restrictions, notably of prices, seen as more pernicious, are treated as *per se* restrictions and other types of agreement not within that category are treated as "reasonable" restraints of trade unless there is an overriding consideration which leads one to the opposite conclusion.

Initially, of course, Community law did not go down that route because in Article 85(1) and (3), as with the RTPA, the approach to justification was to say "it is the administrative authorities who give the exemption". In other

words, we will adopt a wide interpretation of Article 85 but we will exempt
either by block exemption or by individual decisions. Of course, as time
passed, that was not seen as a complete solution, partly because the
adoption of exempting regulations dealing with notifications and so on and
so forth was itself a complex, timeconsuming and laborious job, and partly
because, however well-intentioned the system of exemption, you cannot
foresee and deal with every foreseeable type of case. So little by little,
without really ever admitting it, it can perhaps be said that Community law
is itself now developing its own rule of reason, with the general effect that
certain restraints in certain agreements are not to be regarded as restrictions
of competition within the meaning of Article 85(1). For example, in the very
early *Société Technique Minière* v. *Maschinenbau Ulm GmbH* [2] case an
exclusive agreement where exclusivity is necessary to permit a trader,
possibly a relatively small trader, to take the risk of opening up a new
market is not regarded by the Court as necessarily a restriction of competition within Article 85(1) requiring exemption.

Later cases concerning patent licences in *Nungesser (LC) KG & Kurt
Eisele* v. *Commission*,[3] concerning franchise agreements in *Pronuptia de
Paris GmbH* v. *Pronuptia de Paris Irmgard Schillgallis*,[4] concerning
covenants upon the sale of a business in *Remia BV & Verenigde Bedrijven
Nutricia BV* v. *Commission*,[5] and more recently at the level of the CFI in
the Perfumes cases *Leclerc* v. *Commission*,[6] a number of "restrictive provisions" were seen as ancillary restraints to some procompetitive object and
were not regarded as falling within Article 85(1).

One of the conundrums of competition law, is to see how far this "rule
of reason" approach goes. Because if you take it to a logical destination
you hardly need, or you need much less, exemption. You can bring a great
number of things under a rule of reason. And of course this problem is at
its most acute in the common case of an agreement that is apparently full
of all kinds of restrictions, but that permits something to happen that
would not otherwise have happened. The classic example is the patent
licence whereby, had the patentee not granted a licence, the patent would
not be worked by the licensee. Is the fact that the licensee, in working that
licence, is subject to restrictions, to be regarded as "a restriction on competition", given that without the licence in the first place he would not be
trading at all? These are philosophical and conceptual problems to which
most systems of competition law have not yet found an answer.

More acute in the joint venture field, upon which there is the CFI's
judgment in *European Night Services Ltd (ENS) and others* v. *Commission
of the European Communities*,[7] is the problem of how you analyse a collab-

[2] Case 26/65 [1966] ECR 235.   [3] Case 258/78 [1982] ECR 2015.
[4] Case 161/84 [1986] ECR 353.   [5] Case 42/84 [1985] ECR 2545.
[6] Case T-19/92 [1996] ECR II-1851.
[7] Joined Cases T–374, 375, 384 & 388/94, judgment of 15 Sept. 1998.

oration between competitors to achieve a result that none of them is able to achieve by themselves. They all accept restrictions in the interest of creating a joint venture, and they aim to achieve a result; without the restrictions they could not achieve a result which is in itself pro-competitive.

How do you analyse that? Do you have a wide test which says that everything which looks in legal terms like a restriction is treated as a restriction but we exempt it? Or do you have a narrow test which says, well this is not really a restriction because nobody in their right mind would say it has a restrictive effect in that market context? We will treat it under a rule of reason as falling outside the idea of an agreement restricting or preventing competition. Now it is very hard to speculate, and the Act as far I can see goes down the EC approach, of providing for various exemptions and so forth, building on the existing EC model.

But if you take a 20-year perspective, all I would say is that it cannot be ruled out that over time the European Community will evolve more towards the other approach, and say that more and more things do not fall within Article 85 in the first place upon the basis of some kind of rule of reason analysis, in order further to reduce the administrative burden and the legislative difficulty of legislating for every kind of procompetitive agreement that you want to preserve. It remains to be seen, and I simply say that this is a very important area upon which some reflection is necessary.

Of course, I have now wandered rather away from the RTPA where we started. Perhaps before completely leaving that I would only say that the authors of the RTPA did achieve what they set out to do, the decartelisation of manufacturing industry and, in the 1980s, of some sevices. The most spectacular result, which with the benefit of hindsight can be traced directly to the RTPA, was the Big Bang in the City of London which came about effectively because of the 1973 amendment of the RTPA which brought services legislation into the scope of those Acts. That necessitated the registration of the Stock Exchange rulebook. That rulebook was defended before the Restrictive Practices Court. The government became extremely concerned that this case was risking destabilising the City. It then passed an Act of Parliament which took the Stock Exchange agreement outside the RTPA, but only on certain conditions: that the Stock Exchange abandon certain rules concerned with the payment of fixed commissions and the operation of the market. And as the Stock Exchange itself had argued in that case, the abandonment of those rules brought about a radical change, whether for good or ill is not for me to opine. But it did bring about a radical change, and the result was the end of the club, the old City club, and the renewal of the City of London which has been a dynamic and successful enterprise ever since. And that is not a bad achievement for the legislation that we are now quietly placing at rest and repealing in this Act.

To go on, of course, and to come now to another reflection which is essentially "internationalisation". The old RTPA was based on the idea of United Kingdom public interest and on the idea that one was just looking at, effectively, the United Kingdom. Of course, the world has changed since then and we have global markets. Almost all the major countries have modern competition legislation, much of it is modelled on Article 85 and 86, not only in more or less the whole of Europe—with the exception of Germany, which has its own slightly more formal legislation, one year older than the RTPA—but also in other parts of the world including South America and Africa. The effect of this is, I think, that it is quite right that UK legislation is brought into line with the general trend. Indeed, in my closing time at the Bar I was once asked to advise whether the RTPA had now become illegal because it was so different from everybody else's legislation and the requirement of the public register was, in itself, an obstacle to the free movement of goods and freedom of trade within the Community. I never, fortunately, had to argue that particular point of view, but at least it was one that was being put at the time.

Now in this international context there are two strengths I think to be derived from this new Competition Act, and it is going to be very interesting to see how it works out. The first is that the Community institutions, particularly the Commission, are finding it very difficult to cope by themselves with all the problems that are thrown up by competition policy and therefore some kind of system whereby the laws of the Member States are similar to the Community laws, if not identical, and are operated on broadly similar lines should enable, in a welcome application of the principle of subsidiarity, more to be done at the local coal-face in a way that is probably better adapted to local traditions, leaving the Commission free to deal with matters that really do have a European dimension. This will also have the apparently selfish result from the point of view of the CFI that the difficult cases where the complainant is told to go away because there is no "Community interest" in his complaint, so therefore the Commission is justified in not taking it, may become somewhat easier to handle if one knows that at a local level there is an effective national administration that can take up the complaint. It has been, I think, a lacuna at least in the British situation for some time that Brussels has been seen as a more effective complaints machinery than Chancery Lane, and that if something can be done to reverse that situation, so much the better.

The second advantage that I would identify is that it is a twoway train. Just as in other areas, for example in the Convention for the Enforcement of Judgments, the European Court will pay very high regard to decisions of the national courts in particular areas, I am quite sure that, as the British authorities gain experience and take decisions, those decisions will in themselves have an impact well beyond the national context and will be taken into account and used and followed in other Community countries and up to the highest level. Anecdotally, having recently had to grapple with the problem of the selective distribution of perfumes, I can say that one would have risked becoming lost in what the issues really were and what possible approaches to the problem might have been, had not the MMC done a full enquiry in that particular industry. The results of this enquiry were made available to us (and relied on, curiously, by all parties to the case, to support opposite conclusions,) but nonetheless provided source material that was invaluable in struggling to reach a conclusion. So from the international point of view all this is to be welcomed.

Perhaps in that context it is worth saying something about balance. Very often competition law is not black and white. It is very often about balancing interests. Many very successful economies, have been based historically on cartelisation: Germany until 1914, Japan until comparatively recently, the Netherlands until comparatively recently. All these are countries which have got on extremely well without any kind of competition law. And not all restrictive agreements are necessarily bad. Indeed, at the extreme, competition carries with it the seed of its own destruction, as the efficient firm will drive out its rivals and arrive at a position of perceived dominance. In such a situation the wisdom of Judge Learned Hand in the *Alcoa*[8] case of 1946 is relevant: "The successful competitor, having been urged to compete, should not be turned upon when he wins". Again, perceived dominance may not exist, or may not matter very much if one looks at the timescale. Perhaps the most striking example in recent times is that of *IBM* v. *Commission*[9] where Jeremy Lever QC, Judge David Edward and John Swift QC, to name but a few of those present today, argued in the early 1980s that IBM was not dominant and that consequently no regulatory measures were necessary, a contention that some regarded as almost risible at the time. But within five years the argument was proved to be correct—the perceived dominance of IBM, which effectively disappeared under a welter of new products, innovations, PCs, desktop computers and so forth, was in fact much more apparent than real. In putting into effect this legislation a sense of perspective and a sense of ability to apply common sense is necessary.

I think to close I shall just take a few more points. The first point is this, that I would myself respectfully challenge or at the least qualify the title of this Conference which is: "The Europeanisation of Community Competition Law". First, it is not entirely accurate historically. At common law, price agreements and certain other restrictive agreements were always illegal. That tradition, that body of case law, crossed the Atlantic in the eighteenth and nineteenth centuries and was taken up in the Sherman Act of the United States. And if you look to the reports of Congress in relation to the adoption of that Act, the legislators (the

[8] *US* v. *Aluminum Co. of America* 148 F. 2d 416 (2nd Cir. 1945).
[9] Case 60/81 [1981] ECR 2639.

members of Congress) thought they were enacting the common law of
England. Back in England the common law did not develop any further,
beyond the point it reached in 1898. But the American legislators took it
further. Then came a long period of strife, war, recession, depression,
tariff barriers and so forth. But after the Second World War when the
Americans were again, by force of circumstances, taking a close interest in
European affairs, the Sherman Act concepts were reintroduced in the
allied decartelisation laws in Germany after the war. Then they said you
must put into your new treaty a Sherman Act-type provision, which
became Article 65 of the ECSC Treaty, which became in turn Article 85 of
the EC Treaty, which now in turn becomes a section of the Competition
Act of 1998, symetrically following an almost 100 year route back to
where it started.

But perhaps more seriously, on this question of Europeanisation, there
are two points to make. One is that the European system, despite its
apparent differences, is not as different as you may think because there is a
fundamental similarity and familiarity: Community law is a case law
system. That is to say, and this is particularly true of the competition law
area,—the law itself is developed on a case-by-case basis, which is exactly
the same principle that the common law has followed for many years.
Anybody familiar with a case law system should be entirely at home
within such a system, though to some continental lawyers, particularly
those of the traditional civil law school, it may be somewhat unfamiliar—
there being no detailed Code to offer guidance.

And secondly, there are not going to be entirely similar problems under
the British system. Much of EC law is driven by the need for market
integration. Sometimes there are rules that are adopted for reasons that
seem rather obscure. Perhaps to achieve "fairness" to a certain group of
traders like motor vehicle dealers. Perhaps for other reasons that are to do
with political considerations. So that not everything that has so far been
adopted in the Community context is necessarily adaptable to the British
context.

Finally, I think, procedure. Of course, it is interesting for me particularly
to look at the appellate provisions of this Act, in particular the Competition
Appeals Tribunal, which I am not equipped to say anything about in detail.
But there is one very important difference which I welcome and which I will
make as a final comment, which is this. Under the EC Treaties, the so-called
"appeal" to the CFI is not an appeal. It is a judicial review based on the
grounds set out under Article 173 of the Treaty which are, effectively, procedural failure, lack of competence, error of law or misuse of powers. Those
bare provisions have been amplified over the years in case law and much
reliance has been placed on the duty to give reasons and the Court has had
no difficulty in controlling, in detail, material error of fact and material
error of law, so that the judicial review as operated by the CFI has perhaps

become more detailed as time has gone on. But nonetheless, and particularly in the area when one comes to the discretion of the Commission—the discretion to exempt, the discretion to impose certain conditions, the question of how one balances particular economic advantages and particular economic detriments—one has left a margin of appreciation, perhaps a diminishing margin, but nonetheless a real margin of appreciation to the Commission so that if the Commission has gone wrong all one can do is send it back for the decision to be retaken. The difference I think with the appeal tribunal, which brings us, I am happy to say, in line with Paris and Berlin, is that the appeal tribunal has a full jurisdiction over all matters of fact, law and penalty. That should enable a more flexible and more appropriate judicial review to take place of decisions of the Director, should the need arise.

2

The OFT's Role in the New Regime

MRS MARGARET BLOOM*,[1]

Introduction

Early in 1998 I spoke at a seminar on the Competition Bill which Christopher Bellamy was chairing. He ended his introductory talk with a most apposite but succinct summary of the challenges of the new regime. These were:

- how to deliver legal certainty with an effects based regime;
- how to catch anti-competitive agreements and practices without catching harmless ones;
- how to ensure fair procedures without introducing cumbersome and slow ones; and
- how to ensure an effective competition regime without undue regulatory burdens on business and cost to the authorities.

These are the same challenges which we are seeking to meet at the OFT in implementing the new regime. This is the most important reform of competition law since the creation of the OFT 25 years ago. It is a reform which we warmly welcome. We intend to ensure it is a success. All our preparations are essentially aimed at securing the right balance in respect of the above objectives. These are far from easy challenges. However, in aiming to meet them we have benefited greatly from advice from other competition authorities and from all those responding to our invitations to comment on draft published material. We are also benefiting from the direct experience which our various secondees from law firms have of handling cases involving Articles 85 and 86. This chapter discusses the preparations and plans for our new role in terms of:

- guidelines for the application and enforcement of the new legislation and guidance on penalties;

---

* Director of Competition Policy, Office of Fair Trading.
[1] The views expressed in this chapter are personal and are not necessarily those of the DGFT.

- our proposed education programme on the new legislation and advice on compliance;
- procedural rules and our internal procedures;
- powers of investigation;
- institutions; and
- transitional arrangements.

A survey conducted by *Global Competition Review* in March 1998 of "95 top competition lawyers and economists" reported that 79 per cent "are comfortable with the powers given to the OFT under the Bill". However only 52 per cent agreed that "the OFT and MMC, in its Competition Commission format, [will] be able to change their decision-making processes sufficiently to permit legal scrutiny". While the first result is an encouraging vote of confidence, the second indicates one of the areas where we need to consider our procedures carefully—but not at the cost of introducing ones which are cumbersome and slow or impose undue regulatory burdens.

The rate of development at OFT is moving at a fair pace. I am conscious that by the time this chapter is presented some further changes may have taken place—this will be even more marked by the time that the chapter is published.

Guidelines and Guidance on Penalties

The Act requires the DGFT to provide advice and information about the application of the prohibitions (section 52), guidance on penalties (section 38) and procedural rules (section 51).

Guidelines Providing Advice and Information

The guidelines are to explain the new prohibitions "to persons who are likely to be affected by them" and "to indicate how the Director expects [the] provisions to operate". Hence, the guidelines are being prepared for business rather than legal specialists, although they are clearly of considerable interest to the latter also. Indeed, many of the most useful comments which have been made on the drafts issued so far have come from legal specialists. In preparing the guidelines we are working with the sector regulators who have concurrent powers with the DGFT in their particular areas. The draft guidelines are being issued jointly by the DGFT and the regulators. In due course, some of the sector regulators may issue additional guidelines to cover aspects of particular concern to the companies which they regulate. These additional guidelines will, though, all be part of the same series.

We have published nine drafts (*The Major Provisions, Market Definition, De Minimis, Dual Notifications, EC "Comfort" Letters, Transitional Arrangements, The Chapter I Prohibition, The Chapter II Prohibition* and *Concurrent Application to Regulated Industries*) for consultation. Annex A lists the subjects which are currently expected to be covered in guidelines. The guidelines are published on the OFT website[2] but it is also possible to obtain a paper version if access to an electronic one is not easy.

Consultation on the draft guidelines is important. The DGFT is required under the Act to consult "such persons as he considers appropriate" in preparing the guidelines. Hence a formal consultation process will also be required after Royal Assent. This will be for those guidelines which are ready by then, which may not cover the full list of subjects in Annex A. However, the key guidelines for applying the legislation will be ready by then.

One of the objectives of the guidelines is to ensure that as far as possible business understands the new legislation and therefore avoids anti-competitive agreements and practices.

Another objective is to enable those who suffer from anti-competitive behaviour to recognise such behaviour and make a complaint to the OFT or a regulator. Yet another objective is to advise business on when it is necessary to notify agreements to the authorities and, equally importantly, when it is not necessary to notify us. On the third objective, our current forecast is that we will receive around 600 requests annually for guidance and around 400 for decisions[3] under Chapter I in steady state operation of the new regime after the prohibition has bedded in. We expect very few notifications under Chapter II. In addition, we anticipate about 1,200 complaints annually under Chapters I and II together, with around a quarter of these proving to be sufficiently serious to lead to an investigation. These estimates are based on a survey of law firms and our experience with filings and complaints under the current legislation. For comparison, the DGIV figures for 1997 are 221 notifications, 177 cases opened following complaints and 101 cases opened on the Commission's own initiative. DGIV made 27 formal decisions and closed 490 cases by informal procedures. Its total input of cases was 499 in 1997, total output 517 and end-of-year stock of cases 1,262.

Only agreements with an appreciable effect on competition will be caught by the Chapter I prohibition. We suspect that if we do receive as many as 1,000 notifications a good proportion of them will be unnecessary as they are unlikely to be for agreements with an appreciable effect on competition. Also some might be for agreements which are not caught by

---

[2] *http://www.oft.gov.uk/html/new/guides.htm*

[3] These estimates were significantly reduced subsequently as a result of the exclusion of vertical agreements and the OFT campaign to discourage unnecessary notifications.

the prohibition because of exclusions or block exemptions. It is unlikely that such cases would receive a formal decision or guidance—rather we may issue a letter explaining that the agreement does not have an appreciable effect on competition or is covered by an exclusion or block exemption. The draft guideline on *de minimis* stated that the DGFT would be unlikely to consider that an agreement has an appreciable effect on competition unless the parties have a share of the relevant market in excess of 20 per cent.[4] We are keen to be able to concentrate resources on the areas of highest priority, such as cartels, establishing precedents and processing efficiently those agreements which genuinely need a decision or guidance. We are, also, keen to encourage complaints as these will be the prime source of information on cartels and other anti-competitive activity. Although we are expecting to have around 50 extra staff in due course, if we receive many unnecessary notifications this will inevitably lead to undesirable delays.

Dual notifications to both DGIV and OFT for agreements which "may affect trade between Member States" are another category of notifications where we hope the guideline will discourage unnecessary notifications. Many agreements will be subject to both Community and national law as the rubric "may affect trade between Member States" is interpreted very widely by DGIV and the Community courts. In many cases we consider it will be preferable for the parties to such agreements to notify DGIV rather than the OFT because:

– notification to DGIV gives provisional immunity under both Article 85 and Chapter I until DGIV has made a determination. But, notification to OFT cannot provide immunity against Article 85;
– agreements which have an individual EC exemption, which benefit from an EC block exemption or would have so benefited if they had affected trade between Member States are all exempt from the Chapter I prohibition. But, Chapter I exemptions cannot provide exemption from Article 85; and
– the Act provides for backdating of exemptions to Chapter I prior to the date of notification unlike the position under Regulation 17, which does not generally, currently allow backdating for exemptions to Article 85. Backdating might be required under Chapter I where nullity of an agreement is an issue in a court case.

Those agreements with reasoned comfort letters from DGIV covering either Article 85(3) exemption or negative clearance (because they do not have an appreciable effect on competition) will be relatively low priority for OFT and we suggest these should not normally be notified to us. However, this does not apply in the case of negative clearance comfort letters which are on the basis of no effect on trade between Member States.

[4] Subsequently increased to 25 percent in final guidelines.

Guidance on Penalties

Section 38 requires the DGFT to produce guidance on the appropriate amount of any penalties for approval by the Secretary of State. After consulting the Secretary of State on the form of publication, the DGFT may chose how he will publish the guidance. As with the guidelines, the guidance will be prepared in consultation with the regulators. A formal, public consultation will be required following Royal Assent.

Following proposals by the Opposition in the House of Lords, an amendment was made (now section 38(3)) in the House of Commons so that the DGFT (and regulators) may impose a penalty for infringing the prohibitions "only if he is satisfied that the infringement has been committed intentionally or negligently by the undertaking". This is, of course, the same position as under Regulation 17.

Interestingly, section 38(9) states that "If a penalty or a fine has been imposed by the [European] Commission, *or by a court or other body in another Member State*, in respect of an agreement or conduct, the Director, an appeal tribunal or the appropriate court must take that penalty or fine into account when setting the amount of a penalty" (emphasis added). The requirement to take account of a penalty imposed in another Member State is unusual, possibly unique.

The DGFT has stated that he is likely to take into account the existence of a compliance programme in determining the amount of penalty to be imposed on a company found to have infringed the law. However, just having a programme is unlikely to be sufficient to mitigate a penalty if it has not been actively implemented, evaluated and regularly audited. Also, the DGFT may consider the existence of past Restrictive Practices Court orders or undertakings *in lieu* when assessing the level of penalty appropriate for similar anti-competitive activities infringing the Chapter I prohibition.

Education and Compliance

The success of the new regime will depend materially upon the extent to which business is aware of the implications of the new law. Hence we are developing an education programme for companies, businesses, trade associations and other representative bodies. This will be launched after Royal Assent. The programme will entail a number of elements. One will be the publication of a series of short booklets which summarise the new legislation in straightforward language. These will be in addition to the formal guidelines required under the Act. Another element will be seminars which we hope will be organised by the CBI, the Institute of Directors, chambers of commerce, trade associations and similar bodies.

OFT staff will be available to talk at these events about the new legislation and about compliance.

As with the issue of guidelines, the aim of the education programme is to ensure that more businesses will abide by the new law and to encourage those who suffer from anti-competitive activity to complain to the OFT or the regulators. Our current forecast is that we will receive over 200 complaints under Chapter I and around 1,000 under Chapter II. One of the booklets will provide advice on how to make a complaint.

We are planning to provide general advice on compliance programmes. We have consulted the Australian, US and Canadian competition authorities and DGIV, all of which have very relevant experience of advising business on compliance programmes. US companies, in particular, take compliance very seriously. The Canadian Competition Bureau recently issued guidance on features which it considers essential to maximise conformity with its Competition Act. We have also looked into some of the programmes which are already being operated by businesses here.

Current OFT thinking is that the following elements should be included as a minimum in an effective compliance programme:

– *support of senior management*: this needs to include visibly active involvement of directors and senior management in the programme;
– *appropriate compliance policy and procedures*: both the policy and procedures must be communicated in a suitable format—such as a handbook—to all employees whose business dealings may have competition law implications, and updated as necessary;
– *training*: this can take a variety of forms including informal seminars, video presentations and one-off training exercises such as mock "dawn raids". One company recently commissioned a firm of city lawyers to arrange a mock DGIV raid which most of the staff, including senior staff, thought was genuine. I understand that this was very effective in alerting staff to EC competition law; and
– *evaluation*: effective evaluation is essential and may involve informal feedback sessions with employees as well as formal audits.

The DGFT has recommended that all businesses should consider what is required to comply with the new law. The precise make-up of a compliance programme will depend on the nature of the business in question; what is suitable for one company may not be suitable for another.

A booklet on compliance will be issued as part of the education programme. However, OFT will not be endorsing individual company programmes. We will not have the resources for this; an endorsement today might not be appropriate tomorrow as the business may change; also, the DGFT should not fetter his discretion to assess compliance programmes when fixing penalties.

Procedural Rules and Internal Procedures

The first step in developing the procedural rules has been to develop OFT's internal Procedures Manual.

Internal Procedures

In developing our procedures we have drawn on DGIV's Procedures Manual, extensive advice from other competition authorities and the experience of our secondee lawyers with Article 85 and 86 cases. In addition we have benefited from our experience of conducting competition assessments modelled on Article 85 under the Producer Responsibility Obligations (Packaging Waste) Regulations 1997 (SI 1997/648).

We have addressed many issues including the future role and training of case officers, the new structure of the Competition Policy Division, the IT required for the case management system and the transitional arrangements. The following is a brief description of the current position on some of these issues.

Case officers: there will be a move away from the current situation whereby cases are handled by generalist case officers supported as necessary by specialist advice from lawyers and economists to a system in which cases are handled by case officers who have been trained in economics and law. Staff who take on this role may currently be working as generalists or as specialist economists or have a legal qualification. Specialist support from lawyers and economists will continue to be provided, but this will only be necessary for more complex legal and economic issues. Existing staff and those joining to work on the new legislation will require fairly extensive training. We are in the process of tendering for a substantial training programme so that all case officers will be expert in both economics and law. The planned level of special expertise will be to diploma standard and will be in addition to the normal requirement for these posts of at least a university first degree. In the longer term, our aim is to devise a training programme for case officers that leads to an externally recognised qualification. The sector regulators may wish to take part in this training programme.

The structure of the Competition Policy Division: we are currently planning to have a Policy Branch similar to Directorate A in DGIV, Merger Branch, Cartels Branch and a number of Sectoral Branches. The aim of establishing a Cartels Branch is to ensure that resources are available for pursuing cartels. In some other regimes, the work on cartels suffered when the volume of notifications overwhelmed staff. Complaints will be handled by the relevant Sectoral Branch unless they involve a cartel.

IT for case management system: a tender for the new system was put out in the *Official Journal of the European Communities* in July.

Procedural Rules

Section 51 and schedule 9 provide for procedural rules, for example, covering the procedures and a timetable for decision-making and the information required from parties on notification. The rules must be approved by an order made by the Secretary of State before they come into operation. The draft rules will have been out for consultation well before the conference. They are streamlined, where appropriate, with DGIV rules in order to minimise burdens on business, for example, our Form N is similar to Form A/B. A draft of Form N has been on the OFT website for some months. There is no timetable in this first version of the rules. Mr McCartney stated in Commons Committee session that the timetable will be introduced "once the regime has bedded down". However, we will aim to work to an administrative timetable from the start.

The Director's rules cannot depart from the high level principles of Community law which are imported under section 60. However, the Director's rules and the Tribunal rules should be taken together to determine whether the Act gives effect to these high level principles. There is no exhaustive list of high level principles of Community law. They include the principles of fairness, legal certainty and proportionality. The Director's rules need not be consistent with the procedural rules and practices established by the European Commission. Procedural rules and practices are not imported under section 60.

Mr McCartney stated in Commons Committee session that consideration of the question of oral hearings needs to take account of the fact that the appeal system under the Act is superior to that under EC law. Under the Act, the Appeal Tribunal will conduct a full rehearing on the merits of the case and can substitute its decision (e.g. on the grant of an exemption) for that of the Director. The Court of First Instance is confined, at least in theory, to reviewing Commission decisions on judicial review type grounds. Mr McCartney further stated that he would not necessarily expect the Director's rules to convey an absolute right to an oral hearing, though the Director might want to permit an oral hearing if requested.

Powers of Investigation

The ease with which agreements can be concealed under the present legislation has made it difficult to uncover and act against seriously anti-competitive cartels. The procedures under the Restrictive Trade Practices Act (RTPA) are cumbersome and lengthy; for example, it recently took nine years to conclude a case against ready-mixed concrete cartels. The lack of adequate powers of investigation is a particular weakness. Currently, we can enter premises and collect evidence when empowered to act on behalf of the European Commission but cannot do so to investigate national cases. Adequate powers of investigation are key to the effectiveness of the new legislation.

The powers of investigation are in sections 25–31 and 42–44. The DGFT (and regulators) will be able to investigate where he has "reasonable grounds for suspecting" that a prohibition has been infringed compared with "reasonable cause to believe" under the RTPA. The latter has proven to be a difficult threshold to satisfy.

The DGFT will have power to enter premises—unannounced where necessary—to take copies of documents and to require explanations. The DGFT will have the power to enter premises, using force where necessary, and to search the premises, on authority of a warrant. This is a procedure based on that in the Companies Act, except that warrants are to be from a High Court judge rather than a magistrate. The amendment to the High Court was made in the House of Lords following proposals from OFT, CBI and others. Obstructing the DGFT's right of entry, deliberately supplying false or misleading information, destroying or concealing information and failing to comply with a requirement imposed under the investigatory powers (e.g. failing to produce a document) will be criminal offences.

A variety of views has been expressed on the new powers of investigation. Some have welcomed the powers strongly. Some have questioned them. Some have suggested the powers should be further strengthened, in particular, to include a general power to interrogate persons who might be able to provide information. This power would have been analogous to that conferred on DTI inspectors under the Companies Act.

Interesting amendments and statements made in Parliament include the following. There was an amendment made in the House of Lords to ensure that a genuine inability to provide an explanation of a document will not be an offence. In response to concerns about legal privilege, Lord Simon explained that under section 30 legal privilege extends to in house lawyers, in contrast to the position under Community law. Another government statement was that the Act provides the same defence against self-incrimination as under Community jurisprudence and set out in the *Orkem* case. In the House of Commons, Mr McCartney stated that the rights of undertakings to obtain legal advice when subject to investigation will be in the Director's rules and that this will follow DGIV practice. Their practice is for investigators to wait a limited time for lawyers to arrive, but only if the investigators remain on the premises to ensure that records remain untouched.

The new powers will bring us broadly into line with the investigatory powers of other Member States. The UK is currently the only Member State with no powers to make on-site inspections. The new powers are, of course, significantly weaker than those in the USA and Canada with their criminal investigatory powers, such as the impanelling of a grand jury and the use of FBI covert investigations, to discover criminal anti-trust violations. At the same time as when the Bill was passing through Parliament, the Canadians introduced a Bill into their Parliament which included telephone tapping powers for their Competition Bureau.

The powers of investigation are modelled on those of the European Commission under Regulation 17. However, in contrast to the powers in the Act, the Commission has no powers to direct its investigatory efforts against individuals nor powers to obtain search warrants. But, the Commission can, of course, request the assistance of Member State authorities to conduct on-site inspections. Indeed, the Act makes provision for search warrants to assist the Commission and for sanctions against individuals who intentionally obstruct the exercise of these powers under a warrant (sections 61–65).

It is not intended that the prohibitions and the retained complex monopoly and scale monopoly provisions should be used in parallel on the same matters. Where there is a suspected infringement of the prohibitions, it should be expected that it will be pursued under the powers in the Act rather than using the monopoly provisions. The complex monopoly provisions are retained for activities which are not caught by the prohibitions, while the scale monopoly provisions are intended for dealing with an abuse which is likely to recur due to structural deficiencies in a market. The Act (sections 66 and 67) amends the Fair Trading Act 1973 to strengthen the DGFT's investigatory powers in relation to complex and scale monopolies.

Institutions

Apart from the OFT, the other institutions with a significant role in the new regime are those sector regulators with concurrent powers with the DGFT in their particular areas and the new Competition Commission.

Sector Regulators

Section 54 and Schedule 10 of the Act provide for concurrent powers for the telecommunications (OFTEL), electricity (OFFER), gas (OFGAS), water (OFWAT), rail (ORR) and Northern Irish electricity and gas (OFREG) regulators. It is important to ensure that consistent decisions will be made by all these bodies in applying the prohibitions. How will this be ensured?

– It is anticipated that the vast majority of decisions taken under the new prohibitions will be those made by the DGFT rather than the regulators because of the much greater jurisdictional coverage of the former then the latter. It is the decisions which will drive the case law.
– The Act is drafted to ensure that decisions taken will be consistent with

those which would have been taken in handling a similar Community case. The "governing principles" section (section 60) will apply whether decisions are taken by a regulator or the DGFT.

– The OFT and the regulators will consult before taking action on a matter which may be covered by the concurrent powers. Generally, the regulators will deal with cases in their jurisdiction rather than the DGFT.
– The OFT and the regulators will be bound by one set of procedural rules. These include a single notification point for guidance or decision on agreements at OFT. There is provision to draft further rules, if necessary, covering arrangements for handling concurrency.
– There is one set of guidelines. The OFT chaired Concurrency Working Party oversees the development of the guidelines, rules and other joint issues.
– The system of appeals is common for cases whether they are handled by the sector regulators or the DGFT.

The merger powers remain reserved to the OFT, although the regulator is always consulted by us on utility mergers and the practice has developed of the regulator undertaking the majority of the public consultations.

Competition Commission

The Competition Commission (section 45, Schedule 7) will take over the existing functions of the Monopolies and Mergers Commission which becomes the Monopolies and Mergers Committee (MMC). The MMC will continue to conduct detailed investigations: mergers, references under sector regulators licence regimes and a reduced number of monopoly references. The new Appeal Tribunal in the Competition Commission will hear appeals against decisions of the DGFT and the sector regulators under the prohibitions (sections 46–49, Schedule 8). This new tribunal function will be scrutinised by the Council on Tribunals.

The Tribunal will be more court like while retaining flexibility to deal with cases speedily. The President of the Tribunal (Schedule 7) will need to be legally qualified, as will those members of the tribunal panel qualified to chair individual tribunals. The Secretary of State, who appoints the President in consultation with the Lord Chancellor, must be satisfied in selecting the President that he has "appropriate experience and knowledge of competition law and practice".

Appeals to the Tribunal will be on the full merits of the case, that is a full rehearing. As stated above, this is wider than under the EC system where appeals are limited to judicial review type grounds. This is a potentially far-reaching difference from the structure of European institutions and should mean less focus on procedural matters and more on substance.

Third parties with a sufficient interest in the DGFT's (or regulator's) decision and bodies representing such persons will also be able to appeal to the Tribunal (section 47). A wider range of third parties will be able to appeal than under the EC system. Appeals beyond the Tribunal lie to the Court of Appeal (and equivalent courts in Scotland and Northern Ireland) on points of law and level of penalty (section 49).

Transitional Arrangements

The transitional arrangements in schedule 13 are important, however they are also detailed and complicated.

They are intended to allow businesses a reasonable time to modify agreements and practices to comply with the new legislation. Consequently, there will be a period of approximately one year ("the interim period") between enactment ("the enactment date")[5] and commencement of the prohibitions ("the starting date").[6] In addition, most agreements made prior to the starting date which comply with existing laws may benefit from certain further concessionary periods of exclusion from the Chapter I prohibition ('transitional periods') running in most cases from the starting date. No transitional periods apply in respect of the Chapter II prohibition. For agreements made in the interim period, it will be possible to obtain guidance prior to the starting date on the application of the Chapter I prohibition ("early guidance").

The Restrictive Trade Practices Act (RTPA) and the Resale Prices Act (RPA) will be repealed as from the starting date. In order to allow firms to concentrate on preparing themselves for the new regime, the RTPA will operate in modified form as regards agreements made in the interim period; in particular, all agreements except price-fixing will be non-notifiable. This will also allow OFT to concentrate on preparing for the new regime.

Among the more significant aspects are the treatment of agreements with directions under section 21(2) of the RTPA, early guidance and the transitional periods. These are discussed below.

Section 21(2) directions: the Act excludes from the Chapter I prohibition all agreements with a direction under section 21(2) of the RTPA. The vast majority of agreements notified to the DGFT under the RTPA receive section 21(2) directions from the Secretary of State that the restrictions or information provisions they contain are not of such significance as to call for investigation by the Restrictive Practices Court. These agreements will not generally be of significance under the new regime and hence are excluded from the Chapter I prohibition. The balance between ensuring an effective competition regime and imposing burdens on business and the OFT

[5] 9 November 1998.
[6] 1 March 2000.

through, for example, a time limited exclusion was considered and, rightly, a permanent exclusion was the outcome. However, the DGFT (or regulator) has a power to claw back this exclusion if he considers the agreement will infringe the prohibition and he is not likely to grant it an exemption. Also, the exclusion is lost if a "material variation" is made to the agreement, for example, converting a joint marketing area into partitioned markets or the addition of a significant competitor as a party to an agreement.

Only registrable agreements made prior to the enactment date and furnished to the OFT within three months are eligible for section 21(2) directions. The agreements must not be non-notifiable under the RTPA. Orders introduced earlier in 1998 significantly extended the categories of non-notifiable agreements under the RTPA. Following their introduction, some law firms encouraged their clients to notify agreements which were no longer notifiable in the hope of securing section 21(2) directions. However, these agreements were returned and the number of filings fell, thereby allowing OFT to concentrate on ensuring that all those agreements eligible for consideration under section 21(2) of the RTPA could be handled by the starting date.

Early guidance: parties to agreements made in the interim period have the option of applying for guidance on whether the agreement is likely to infringe the Chapter I prohibition when it comes into force and, if so, whether exemption is likely. Any early guidance given will have the same effect as guidance which will be available from the starting date, including provisional immunity from penalty. Our best estimate from surveying law firms is that we may receive around 250 notifications for early guidance. The draft transitional guidelines make it clear that agreements should not be notified for early guidance unless they are likely to have an appreciable effect on competition. Notifications for early guidance will be the first opportunity which we will have of assessing whether unnecessary notifications are likely to be made, thereby leading to unnecessary delays.

Transitional periods: the transitional periods are available only for agreements in existence at the starting date; Chapter I will apply immediately to new agreements after that date. The one-year period is the basic rule and the two main types of agreement which are likely to benefit from this period of exclusion from the Chapter I prohibition will be agreements made in the interim period and those made before the starting date to which the RTPA did not apply. Agreements receive no transitional period to the extent to which they are void or unlawfully operated under the RTPA or RPA. There are a few special categories of agreements which receive a five year transitional period.

The effect of the transitional arrangements is likely to be that we shall receive a steady stream of notifications of agreements as they are made after the starting date. A year after the starting date we are likely to receive a substantial number of notifications at the same time. However, given the exclusions in the Act (including the special treatment for vertical and land agreements under section 50) and the careful planning of the transitional arrangements, we are hoping that the impact will not be as serious as that experienced by other European competition authorities with new prohibitions in recent years, such as the Swedish, Irish, Dutch and Danish authorities. The experience of DGIV in the early 1960s is also well known—but that was before block exemptions were introduced.

Conclusion

This chapter has described some of the ways in which the OFT is working to meet the challenges of the new regime. In addition, we are playing a significant role in influencing developments in national and Community law, including the treatment of vertical agreements. These developments will also be of great importance in relation to challenges such as how to catch anti-competitive agreements and practices without catching harmless ones and how to ensure an effective competition regime without undue regulatory burdens on business and cost to the authorities. But these developments are the subject for another chapter.

Annex

Draft list of subjects to be included in guidelines to be issued by the Director General of Fair Trading and sector regulators for telecommunications, gas, electricity, water and railway services. Some of these subjects may be amalgamated into a single, more comprehensive guideline:

The Major Provisions
The Chapter I Prohibition
The Chapter II Prohibition
Market Definition
Powers of Investigation
Concurrent Application to
   Regulated Industries
EC Comfort Letters
Transitional Arrangements
Enforcement
De Minimis
Effects on Mergers and Ancillary
   Restraints

Agreements involving Intellectual
   Property
Vertical Agreements and Restraints
Prohibited Agreements – Land
Interim Measures
Trade Associations and Professional
   Rules
Dual Notifications
The Assessment of Individual
   Agreements and Conduct
Market Power

3

Some Observations on the Civil Consequences of the Chapters I and II Prohibitions

NICHOLAS GREEN QC

Introduction

It is the present intent that the Chapters I and II prohibitions shall give rise to civil consequences in the courts in much the same way as Articles 85 and 86 EC are directly effective and thereby must be given effect to. However, the Chapters I and II prohibitions and Articles 85 and 86 are not identical in their scope or effect. This is self-evident, for example, by reference to the myriad exemptions from the prohibitions set out in the Schedules to the Act. Parliament intends to exempt a host of sectors and professional activities from the prohibitions in circumstances where Articles 85 and 86 would, in principle apply.

The purpose of this chapter is to comment upon some of the "civil" issues which will arise before the courts in relation to the Act, when it comes into force. Two issues, it may be foreseen, may be of particular interest: first, the scope of the guidance clause presently found in section 60 of the Act; secondly, the justiciable scope and effect of the prohibitions themselves.

The Guidance Provision

Section 60 of the Act provides:

"(1 The purpose of this section is to ensure that so far as is possible (having regard to any relevant differences between the provisions concerned), questions arising under this Part in relation to competition within the United Kingdom are dealt with in a manner which is consistent with the treatment of corresponding questions arising in Community law in relation to competition within the Community.

(2) At any time when the Court determines a question arising under this Part,

it must act (so far as is compatible with the provision of this Part and whether or not it would otherwise be required to do so) with a view to securing that there is no inconsistency between:

    (a) the principles applied, and decision reached, by the court in determining that question; and

    (b) the principles laid down by the Treaty and the European Court, and any relevant decision of that Court, as applicable at that time in determining any corresponding question arising in Community law.

(3) The Court must, in addition, have regard to any relevant decision or statement of the Commission.

(4) Sub-sections (2) and (3) also apply to—

    (a) the Director; and

    (b) any person acting on behalf of the Director, in connection with any matter arising under this Part.

(5) In sub-sections (2) and (3), 'court' means any court or tribunal.

(6) In sub-sections (2)(b) and (3), 'decision' includes a decision as to:

    (a) the interpretation of any provision of Community law;

    (b) the civil liability of an undertaking for harm caused by its infringement of Community law."

This is, in many respects, a remarkable section which throws up a number of fundamental issues. One example, which is dealt with below, is whether it operates to endow the Chapters I and II prohibitions with the characteristics, derived from Community jurisprudence, of direct effect and supremacy. If it does so operate it might have remarkable consequences for the relationship between the prohibitions and other provisions of domestic law. Before turning to this issue however, it is desirable to set out a number of observations about the statutory language proposed for the guidance clause.

Section 60(1) contains a mission statement. It states the purpose of the section but does not impose any enforceable obligation upon any relevant court or tribunal. The purpose of the guidance clause is to "ensure" that "questions" arising under this Part (i.e. sections 1–60 inclusive) in relation to competition within the United Kingdom are dealt with in a manner consistent with the treatment of corresponding questions arising in Community law in relation to competition within the Community. The purpose of the guidance provision is thus to secure a stated objective, namely consistency between domestic and Community jurisprudence on corresponding questions. Nice issues of law will, in due course, arise in relation to the scope of this sub-section. What is meant by a "corresponding question" arising in Community law? What is the meaning of "so far as is possible": when will the object of securing consistency prove impossible? It may well be that this latter phrase is designed to cover the fact that the UK Act precludes from the prohibition a large number of sectors and activities, whereas no equivalent exemptions exist from Articles 85 and 86 EC. If an issue arises as to the application of the prohibitions to an exempt sector the fact that such sectors are subject to a prohibition under Community law does not, by that fact alone, mean that the exempt sector becomes so subject under the domestic equivalent simply by virtue of section 60.

Perhaps a more difficult question arises in respect of the importation of the philosophy underlying Articles 85 and 86. It is trite to say that Community competition law is hostile to any form of agreement which seeks to resurrect barriers to trade between Member States. Private undertakings may not, by private agreement, re-create the obstacles to international trade between Member States which other prohibitions in the Treaty seek to address and enjoin. For example, in an exclusive distribution agreement the Community frowns upon attempts to block parallel exports. Such an object is motivated as much by the political philosophy underlying the Community as a whole as by pure micro-economic considerations. However, the same desire to achieve integration does not arise in trade within a single Member State, for example between London and Birmingham. Does section 60 serve to require a court or tribunal to construe the Chapter I prohibition in such a way as to prohibit obstacles to parallel trade between geographic territories within the United Kingdom simply because such is, *prima facie*, prohibited under Article 85? Could it be said that the domestic prohibitions will be construed by reference to prevailing United Kingdom micro-economic policy, as opposed to the corresponding policy existing within the Community as construed by the European Commission and endorsed by the Court of Justice? The considerations which apply at a pan European level are not necessarily those which are germane at the domestic level. The parenthesis in clause 60(1) which states that the purpose of the section is to ensure consistency but "(having regard to any relevant differences between the provisions concerned)" may mean relevant differences not only in the statutory language (i.e. the exemptions) but in the underlying philosophy behind the provisions in question.

Setting aside such problems of construction it is clear that, for the most part, both the Director and those courts or tribunals which are seised of questions arising under Part I of the Act will be bound to look to Community jurisprudence. In this regard the courts are effectively *bound* by decisions of the European Court (which means the Court of Justice and the CFI) but must take Commission decisions as merely persuasive. So far as the latter is concerned section 60(3) states only that courts must "have regard to" relevant decisions or statements of the Commission. As to this, not only will the formal decisions of the European Commission be persuasive but also their "statements", which presumably includes such matters as Article 19(3) Notices pursuant to Regulation 17 and Notices published in the Official Journal setting out Commission guidance and policy on the application of Articles 85 and 86, both generally and in respect of specific sectors.

It is important to note that the domestic courts are required to have regard not only to the jurisprudence of the Community on Articles 85 and 86 but also to the principles laid down by the Treaty. "The Treaty" means the Treaty establishing the European Community: section 59(1). Articles 85 and 86 have given rise to a great deal of jurisprudence. They are also construed in the light of other principles laid down by the Treaty including, in particular, Articles 3(g), 5 and 90. Those provisions plainly enunciate principles laid down by the Treaty. However, it is also strongly arguable that the phrase "principles laid down by the Treaty" includes also the general principles of Community law which are said to arise inferentially out of the Treaty albeit that they are not laid down expressly "in" the Treaty. Use of the word "by" ("principles laid down *by* the Treaty") may extend the operation of the relevant principles to which resort should be had beyond the express language of the Treaty and into the general principles of Community law, which would include those contained in the European Convention on Human Rights. Moreover, and perhaps more significantly from a practical point of view, the "principles laid down by the Treaty" would almost certainly include the twin principles of direct effect and supremacy. If these are incorporated into domestic law they may have significant implications for the relationship between the prohibitions and other provisions of domestic law.

This is a matter to which I return below, but before doing so it is worth observing that in section 60(6) the phrase "decision" (i.e. being that to which resort is bound to be had) includes not only decisions on the interpretation of the provision of Community law but also decisions on "the civil liability of an undertaking for harm caused by its infringement of Community law". As regards the latter point this gives rise to the intriguing possibility that the guidance clause, if operated, will create a form of *renvoi* by reference to the relevant jurisprudence of the Court of Justice which indicates that the conditions under which directly effective rights are to be protected are to be determined according to national law. For instance in *Kerpen* the Court of Justice stated:

> "an agreement falling under the prohibition imposed by Article 85(1) of the Treaty is void and . . . since the nullity is absolute, the agreement has no effect as between the contracting parties. It also follows from the previous judgments of this court . . . that the automatic nullity decreed by Article 85(2) applies only to those contractual provisions which are incompatible with Article 85(1). The consequences of such a nullity or other parts of the agreement are not a matter for Community law. The same applies to any orders and deliveries made on the basis of such agreement and to the resulting financial obligations.
>
> The answer to the second and third questions must therefore be that the automatic nullity decreed by Article 85(2) of the Treaty only applies to those contractual provisions which are incompatible with Article 85(1). The consequences of such a nullity for other parts of the agreement, and for any orders

and deliveries made on the basis of the agreement, and the resulting financial obligations are not a matter for Community law. Those consequences are to be determined by the national court according to its law." [1]

The remainder of this chapter examines the implications of the guidance clause in respect of two issues: first, the issue adverted to above, namely the possible importation into the Chapters I and II prohibitions of the characteristics of direct effect and supremacy; and secondly, the scope of the duties imposed by the Chapters I and II prohibitions and the categories of person entitled to rely thereupon.

Direct Effect and Supremacy

If direct effect and supremacy become characteristics of the Chapters I and II prohibitions then this will have the potential effect of raising those prohibitions into superior obligations taking precedence over inconsistent domestic procedural, judicial or administrative rules which potentially conflict with them. An example where this issue has arisen in the Article 85 context was in *The Society of Lloyd's v. Clementson*.[2] There Lloyd's sought summary judgment for debt against certain Names. The Names counterclaimed on the basis of Article 85(1) and sought to raise the counterclaim as a defence of set off. Impeding the success of the counterclaim was section 14 of the Lloyd's Act 1982 which provided (in summary form) that, subject to certain exceptions which were not relied upon by the Names, Lloyd's was not liable in damages at the suit of the members of the Lloyd's community for negligence or other torts, breach of duty or otherwise in respect of any exercise of, or omission to exercise, any power, duty or function conferred or imposed by the Lloyd's Acts 1871 to 1982 or any bye-law or regulation made thereunder, in so far as, *inter alia*, the underwriting business of any member of the Society or the costs of his membership were affected. If this provision of domestic law was effective, it stood in the way of *any* counterclaim based upon (*inter alia*) Article 85. In the Court of Appeal Sir Thomas Bingham MR stated:

> "If Mr. Clementson is able to establish that Lloyd's has acted in breach of Article 85, then it seems to me at least arguable that he has a good counterclaim for damages on which he is entitled to rely by way of set-off and that section 14 of the Lloyd's Act 1982 cannot be effective to deprive him of that right. If it were otherwise I do not see how national courts could help to enforce the Communities competition regime, as I understand they are expected to do."

That was an example where, at least in principle, the Court of Appeal held

---

[1] Case 319/82, *Société de Venle de Ciments et Bétons de l'est* v. *Kerpen and Kerpen* [1983] ECR 4173, paras. 11 and 12.

[2] [1995] CLC 117.

that a domestic statutory obstacle could not thwart or undermine the effectiveness of a Community right. If the Chapters I and II prohibitions acquire the same ability to have set aside inconsistent domestic judicial, administrative or statutory provisions then that will be a novel characteristic attributed to a domestic statutory provision. Another example of the same characteristic which, on this occasion, was less successful is to be found in the judgment of the Court of Appeal in *Gibbs Mew Plc.* v. *Gemmell.*[3] In that case a landlord of a public house sought possession and judgment for arrears of rent and mesne profits by way of an application for summary judgment pursuant to RSC Order 14. The tenant raised a counterclaim alleging breach of Article 85(1) upon the basis that the beer tie was in breach of that Article and had caused loss to the tenant. The tenant sought to raise the breach of Article 85(1) by way of a defence of set off. The lease contained what has become known as an anti-set off clause pursuant to which the obligation to pay the rent (which obligation of course had been breached and was the basis of the application for possession) was to be paid without deduction abatement or set off. In the purely domestic context of landlord and tenant law the courts have upheld such clauses.[4] However, in the present case the tenant contended that to permit the anti-set off clause to be enforceable was to undermine the directly effective right relied upon by the tenant by way of counterclaim. Peter Gibson LJ rejected this argument:

> "Nor can I accept that [the anti-set off clause] is inconsistent with Community law. It is, of course, correct that Community law insists on the removal of obstacles imposed by Member States to the effective enforcement of directly effective rights: that is the duty of each Member State under Article 5 of the Treaty of Rome. But it does not follow that private parties cannot agree on the exclusion of set-off in a contract. Nor do I see it that such provision can properly be said to be an obstacle to the enforcement of Article 85."

Scope of Duty In Chapters I and II Prohibitions

If Community law constitutes guidance on the scope and effect of the prohibitions then, because of the *renvoi* effect of Community law, judgments of the English courts on the scope and effect of Article 85 will be relevant to the construction of the Chapters I and II prohibitions. In this regard the English courts have, in recent years, grappled extensively with the issue: who may invoke the direct effect of Article 85. The answer which

---

[3] [1998] EuLR 588, *per* Peter Gibson, Schiemann and Mantell LJJ.
[4] See e. g. *Connaught Restaurants Limited v. Indoor Leisure* [1994] 4 All ER 834.

has now been given consistently by the High Court and Court of Appeal is that only third parties (competitors) to agreements may rely upon the direct effect in order to seek relief, but not the co-contractors themselves.

In this regard the courts have taken the view that Articles 85 and 86 are intrinsically different. The latter incorporates a unilateral prohibition on one person, the dominant undertaking. The former imposes a multilateral prohibition on the parties to the agreement or concerted practice in question. In the case of a claim under Article 86 a person contracting with a dominant undertaking who commences proceedings against that undertaking for alleged abuse of a dominant position is not therefore the subject of any prohibition. On the contrary, a co-contractor who sues his counter party for breach of Article 85 is suing upon the basis of a contracted for performance which is prohibited by both parties. Thus, for example, a pub tenant or the licensee of a petrol filling station cannot sue the landlord or supplier on the basis that he was subject to a tie requiring him to purchase his total requirements of beer or fuel from the landlord, supplier or other nominated person. So to do is to sue for the contracted for performance of a clause the performance of which is prohibited by both parties. Plainly, the situation is quite different in the case of a dominant supplier and its customer. The customer may be required, by the dominant supplier, to purchase its entire requirement from that supplier. The customer adheres to the obligation but is prevented from seeking alternative sources of supply. In carrying out its side of the bargain the customer is not performing anything which is unlawful. The same is not true of the supplier, however, who, in imposing and performing the obligation, is abusing a dominant position contrary to Article 86. The distinction between a unilateral and multilateral prohibition is one recognised in English law and which has important practical significance. Thus, for example, in *Phoenix Insurance* v. *Halvanon Insurance* [5] the Court of Appeal stated that where a statute prohibits both parties from concluding or performing a contract when both or either of them have no authority to do so the contract is impliedly prohibited and unlawful. However, where the statute merely prohibits one party from entering into a contract and/or imposes a penalty upon him if he does so (i.e. the unilateral prohibition) it does not *necessarily* follow that the contract is illegal in the hands of the other contracting party. Whether it is or is not may depend upon additional factors such as public policy in the light of the mischief which the statute is designed to prevent, its language, scope and purpose, the consequences for the innocent party and any other relevant considerations.

Another matter affecting the scope and effect of Articles 85 and 86, and therefore the Chapters I and II prohibitions, is the differences in language between the two provisions. Language used in Article 85(1) in enumerating

[5] [1988] 1 QB 216, at 273, 274, *per* Kerr LJ.

examples of agreements which restrict, distort or prevent competition is very similar to the examples of abuse contained in Article 86. However, there are two critical distinctions. Article 86(a) and (b) expressly incorporates notions of "fairness" and "prejudice to consumers". These phrases, which are obviously of considerable significance, are omitted from the equivalent provisions of Article 85(1). The same insertions and omissions are found in the Chapters I and II prohibitions. The particular terms of the two provisions have led the English courts to make a number of observations about the differences between the two prohibitions. In *Chemidus Wavin*[6] Buckley LJ stated:

> "What he is really complaining about is that he has made a bad bargain and, according to him, a thoroughly bad bargain, but I do not think that Article 85 is intended in any way to mend any man's bargains. What it is intended to do is to interfere with distortions of trade. Someone chooses to pay over the odds for some particular item, then I do not think that Article 85 will save him."

This analysis was cited with approval by the Court of Appeal in *IEL* v. *Boyes* .[7]

So, Article 85 is not about bad bargains or, put another way, inequality of bargaining power. Conversely, Article 86 is intrinsically concerned with inequality of bargaining power, which explains the broader ambit of its concerns which stretch beyond purely anti-competitive conduct into exploitative and unfair conduct and conduct which is prejudicial to consumers.

Upon the assumption that the Chapters I and II prohibitions will be construed consistently with the English courts' construction of Articles 85 and 86 EC, then one might expect to see Article 85 giving rise to remedies in favour of third parties/competitors to the contracting parties but not remedies to the contracting parties *inter se*. So far as Article 86 is concerned non-dominant undertakings which are subject to abuse by a dominant undertaking may sue the latter, though there might arise questions as to the circumstances in which even a non-dominant undertaking might be precluded from recovery.

Conclusion

In conclusion, section 60 of the Act raises many interesting questions of law and practice which will undoubtedly tax the courts in the future. In a chapter of this nature it is possible to touch upon only a few such issues. However, these are issues of considerable practical importance and have, in the context of EU competition law, given rise to a great volume of litiga-

---

[6] [1978] 3 CMLR 514.
[7] [1993] 47 EG 140; see also *Gibbs Mew Plc v. Gemmell*, n. 3 above.

tion. Certainly, a good deal of the litigation has concerned vertical agreements which may, in the fullness of time, be excluded from the new Act. Nonetheless, principles devised in the context of those agreements which are of general application to the scope and effect of Articles 85 and 86 will still be relevant to the construction of the new prohibitions even in non-vertical cases.

4

Is More Like Europe Better?: An Economic Evaluation of Recent Changes in UK Competition Policy[1]

Introduction

The 1998 Competition Act represents the most important change in UK competition policy since the 1973 Fair Trading Act. For many years the inadequacies of the existing legislation and procedures have been identified, and proposals for reform put forward. In 1989 the government published a White Paper, *Opening Markets: New Policies on Restrictive Trades Practices*, which proposed replacement of existing legislation with legislation along the lines of Article 85. This was followed in 1992 by a DTI consultation document, *Abuse of Market Power*, which set out options for reforms in areas covered by the Fair Trading Act 1973 and the Competition Act 1980 in respect of anti-competitive behaviour. The document detailed a number of legislative options, and made the case for the introduction of a prohibition of the abuse of dominant positions in markets along the lines of Article 86. In 1996 the DTI published yet another consultation paper, *Tackling Cartels and the Abuse of Market Power*. In respect of restrictive trades practices this accepted the case for Article 85 type legislation, but the government never made room for a bill in the parliamentary timetable, even though it had made a manifesto commitment. In respect of the abuse of market power the consultation

* Jesus College, Oxford, and Institute of Economics and Statistics, Oxford.
[1] At the time of writing (Sept. 1998) the Competition Bill had not yet become an Act, and the Office of Fair Trading had not produced the complete set of drafts of guidelines required under the Act. In particular the draft on vertical agreements had not appeared. Inevitably then, the chapter has to be provisional in some of its analysis and conclusions. I am grateful to Derek Morris and Robin Nuttall for comments on earlier drafts: this should not be taken to imply that they necessarily agree with the arguments presented here.

paper drew back from Article 86 type legislation and contented itself
with proposing some tidying up of existing legislation and procedures. It
was left to a Labour government, in its first year in office, to bring in
legislation for restrictive trades practices along the lines which had been
laid out by the previous administration, and to introduce a tough policy
on anti-competitive behaviour which had been explicitly rejected by its
predecessor.

What then is the overall shape of competition policy in the UK which
emerges from the 1998 Competition Act? In respect of anti-competitive
agreements between firms, the Act introduces a prohibition in a form
which reproduces the wording and substantive content of Article 85. In
respect of abuse of a dominant position, the legislation reproduces Article
86. The application of the legislation is also intended to mirror European
competition policy, and section 60 indicates that European case law will be
normative. The procedures will also be similar. In the UK the Director
General of Fair Trading will act like DGIV in Brussels, with appeals to a
tribunal within the Competition Commission which is intended to have a
similar function to the Court of First Instance. The reason for this close
parallel is not just that the European system is perceived to be better than
the previous UK policy model, but also a desire to simplify things for firms
which are likely to be subject to both regimes. One set of rules will apply
whether the firm is supplying UK markets or European markets. Existing
UK policy with respect to mergers will remain, with references to the
Competition Commission (in its "reporting function" acting essentially as
the old Monopolies and Mergers Commission). This approach is not
dissimilar to the approach to mergers which has developed in Europe in
recent years though the European institutional structure is quite different.
However, *unlike Europe*, UK competition policy will retain, in the form of
the relevant parts of the Fair Trading Act 1973, the capacity to examine
market structures, both scale monopolies and complex monopolies. That
is, the Monopolies and Mergers Commission will continue to report on
such cases as are referred to it by the Secretary of State on the advice of the
Director General of Fair Trading. In summary then, where both Europe
and the UK have equivalent areas of policy action the result of the Act is to
bring the UK into line with Europe, but where Europe lacks a relevant
policy area, as in "structural" questions, then the UK policy retains its
existing instruments.

The issues to be addressed in this chapter are whether this reform of
competition policy in the UK represents a potential (because as much may
depend on the practice as on the formal framework) improvement over
what went on before, and more generally how the reformed policy
measures up to some "ideal" policy framework. The criteria we will apply
are strictly economic: which may seem unduly narrow to some readers, but
has the advantage of focusing attention on key issues.

In a previous paper[2] we developed a set of propositions which in our view should dictate the form and substance of competition policy. The first proposition is that the objective of competition policy should be to promote economic efficiency, rather than competition *per se*, or some wider definition of the public interest. Our defence of this proposition was partly historical: this is the way competition policy has developed, especially in the United States, as the (malign?) influence of economists as expert advisers to the antitrust authorities and to business has grown. But more importantly the proposition reflects the significance attached by successive governments to improving the efficiency of the UK economy, with competition seen as a means to that end.[3] To quote from the Foreword to the DTI consultation document: "[e]ffective and fair competition is essential to ensure value and choice for customers. In the global market place, competition provides a spur to British companies to innovate and invest. Competitiveness both at home and in overseas markets is enhanced by competition in the domestic market. So competition is good for business as well." An emphasis on competition as an incentive for efficiency is a departure from the traditional UK competition policy concern with the "public interest". This is not to say that matters other than competition are unimportant, but that they may be better addressed by other policy instruments. For example, in the debates in Parliament on the Competition Bill, there was considerable discussion about the fate of rural pharmacies: clearly there is an issue here, but it is not primarily a competition issue. If the government wishes to maintain rural pharmacies for social reasons, then the solution may be to subsidise them appropriately. Similarly, the government may have good reasons for wishing to prevent undue concentration of ownership in the media. But the policy to deal with that is not competition policy, unless of course a particular merger or behaviour raises competition issues: rather there should be a separate policy with its own legislation and administration. It should also be recognised that competition and competitive markets will not always be conducive to efficiency. For example a merger may create synergies sufficient to offset any loss of competition in the relevant market. There may then be issues about how to prevent the merged firm from abusing its dominant position, but that does not invalidate the proposition that the net effect in terms of economic efficiency is positive.

Our second proposition was that competition policy should recognise that economic analysis is often ambiguous, *a priori*, about the efficiency effects of particular market structures and conduct. Even in the case of horizontal agreements on prices and outputs between firms in a cartel, the implications of which seem completely clear cut, it has been argued that in

---

[2] D.A. Hay, "Competition Policy", chap. 6 in T. Jenkinson (ed.), *Readings in Microeconomics* (OUP, Oxford, 1996).

[3] Though not the only means: there is, e.g., a role for shareholders in preventing managerial inefficiency or "slack".

particular circumstances ("lumpy" demand in sectors with high fixed costs, and "recession" cartels) agreements may be efficiency enhancing. Other agreements between firms, for example R&D joint ventures, are quite likely to be beneficial to efficiency so long as they are not extended to the marketing of any innovations that may result. Other areas of potential concern for competition policy such as mergers or vertical restraints are even more ambiguous in their effects on efficiency, and may require an inquiry into the precise circumstances of each case.

Our third proposition was that the design of competition policy should reflect this ambiguity of economic analysis. The obvious problem is that an effective competition policy could not do a detailed cost benefit analysis of each and every market situation and firm behaviour. It would not only be expensive in relation to the potential economic gains, but would also undermine what is seen as one of the major virtues of a market system, which is that firms are able to pursue their goals without constantly being subject to scrutiny. They need a set of rules within which they can operate. An important primary element should be criteria for identifying situations where competition is likely to be absent, e.g. market shares of the firms involved. Without some such initial screen the competition authority will be overwhelmed with cases that are probably completely insignificant. The problem with competition rules is that, if framed too restrictively they run the risk of deterring desirable behaviour and, if framed too loosely, the danger of permitting undesirable behaviour. This suggests that competition policy should provide fairly restrictive rules, but give scope for firms to argue a case for exemption from those rules on efficiency grounds. Putting the burden of proof on the firms has the distinct advantage that they have both the incentive to make a case and access to the detailed information on which the case is to be based. Competition policy should also recognise that the incentives for anti-competitive behaviour by firms are very substantial: a successful monopolist or cartel is potentially very profitable indeed. It is therefore essential that a competition policy should have real "teeth" in terms of powers to investigate abuses and impose fines to act as a deterrent, as well as administrative powers to deal with anti-competitive behaviour such as seeking undertakings from a firm not to behave in certain ways or even requiring a firm to divest part of its existing operations. For this there needs to be a public competition authority, though without excluding the possibility of private actions which the experience of the United States has suggested is a useful adjunct to public action. The key feature of the public authority, apart of course from due care in the application of the policy, should be transparency of its decisions. In a market economy the authority has an important role in educating business as to acceptable and unacceptable behaviour, preferably by issuing guidelines. Paradoxically the most successful competition policy authority would be one that did very little, because the rules of the game are clear, the rate of detection of misdemeanours high and the fines punitive, so the firms are careful to behave themselves!

A final proposition addressed the question of harmonisation of competition policies in different economies. In a situation of increasingly international operation by many large firms, it is important the competition policies in different jurisdictions should not be too dissimilar for at least three reasons. The first is that compliance with competition policy rules is costly for international firms, and harmonisation would help to keep those costs down, since the firms would not have to have separate compliance departments for each country in which they were operating. The second is that without harmonisation it is much more difficult to get co-operation between the competition authorities in cases which cross international boundaries. Such cases, especially international cartels or market sharing agreements, are likely to be increasingly important in the future. The third reason is that harmonisation may be an important adjunct to liberalisation of world trade. The concern is that a weak domestic competition policy may be used to protect domestic industry from international competition. For example, the authorities may view benignly the activities of domestic producers in controlling domestic retailing systems to make it difficult for foreign suppliers to enter the market.[4]

In the rest of the chapter we will apply these propositions to the evaluation of UK competition policy as it appears in the aftermath of the Competition Act 1998. For ease of exposition we will consider each broad area of policy in turn: anti-competitive agreements, abuse of dominant positions, vertical restraints and "structural" policies including merger policy. In each area we will ask whether the reforms represent an improvement on what went on before, and whether the reformed policy matches up to the criteria rehearsed above.

Anti-competitive Agreements

Chapter I of the Competition Act 1998 replaces the previous legislation on restrictive trade practices with provisions which are drawn more or less in their entirety from Article 85. Section 2 prohibits agreements which "have as their object or effect the prevention, restriction or distortion of competition within the United Kingdom". Examples include:

"agreements, decisions or practices which—

(a) directly or indirectly fix purchase or selling prices or any other trading conditions;

(b) limit or control production, markets, technical development or investment;

---

[4] See E.M. Graham and J.D. Richardson (eds.), *Global Competition Policy* (Institute for International Economics, Washington, DC, 1997).

(c) share markets or sources of supply;

(d) apply dissimilar conditions to equivalent transactions with other trading parties, thereby placing them at a competitive disadvantage;

(e) make the conclusion of contracts subject to acceptance by the other parties of supplementary obligations which, by their nature or according to commercial usage, have no connection with the subject of such contracts."

Any agreement is to be judged not on the basis of its form (as in the restrictive trade practices legislation) but on the basis of its effects or potential effects on competition. The first three examples are directed at cartel practices of fixing prices, outputs and capacity, and of sharing markets. Examples (d) and (e) are directed at behaviour which, if practised by a dominant firm, might constitute an abuse of a dominant position: the idea is to prevent non-dominant firms agreeing to behave together in an anti-competitive manner. Discussion of these clauses is deferred to the third section of this paper.

The DTI commentary which was published with the draft Bill made clear the intention that the prohibition should only apply to agreements which have a significant or "appreciable" effect on competition. The Director General of Fair Trading is required to interpret the provisions in the light of European precedents on this issue, to avoid any interpretations developing over time which might diverge from European practice. To this end, the Office of Fair Trading has published draft guidelines on *de minimis*, to identify agreements which do not have an "appreciable effect on competition". These refer to the precedent established by the European Court: "an agreement falls outside the prohibition in Article 85(1) where it has only an insignificant effect on the market, taking into account the weak position which the persons concerned have on the market in question".[5] The suggested guidelines refer both to the market share of the parties to an agreement, and to the nature of the agreement. Where the parties' share does not exceed 10 per cent of the relevant market,[6] the view is that agreements will have no appreciable effect on competition. However the nature of the agreement must also be considered: if the agreement involves price fixing, market sharing or agreements to impose minimum resale prices the 10 per cent rule no longer ensures that Chapter I will not be applied. The draft guidelines also indicate some additional considerations to be taken into account, such as the structure of the market, the conditions of entry and the structure of the buyers' side of the market. Slightly oddly, they also note that the Director General 'anticipates that most agreements where market shares fall below 20% will not produce appreciable effects on competition'. Finally there is to be limited immunity for small agreements, where the combined annual turnover of

[5] Case 5/69 *Völk* v. *Vervaecke* [1969] ECR 295.

[6] The views of the OFT on market definition are discussed below in the next part of the chapter.

the parties is below a threshold. Penalties may not be imposed, and the investigation of such agreements will have a low priority. But the Director General still has the right to investigate, and may subsequently remove immunity from penalties.

The draft guidelines on the *Chapter I Prohibition* issued by the Office of Fair Trading are interesting for what they identify as the main targets of this part of the Act. First, the guidelines are concerned only with horizontal agreements, defined as firms that operate at the same level of the production and distribution chain. Vertical agreements are not discussed. The government's intention was that vertical agreements, with the exception of resale price maintenance, should be dealt with under Chapter II or under the "complex monopoly" provisions of the Fair Trading Act 1973, though it did not prove possible to draft the Bill explicitly so as to ensure this division of labour.[7] We return to the question of vertical relationships in markets in the next section. The examples of horizontal agreements given in the draft guidelines contain no surprises: overt collusive agreements, price-fixing, market-sharing, limiting production, limiting or co-ordinating investment, collusive tendering, agreements between purchasers and information agreements. All of these are supported by the European experience in applying Article 85.[8]

Less happily the draft Guidelines are drawn into the question of "concerted practices", which has proved such a contentious issue in Europe. The difficulties with the concept can be identified by reference to two key judgments of the European Court, both of which are quoted in the guidelines. In the first, the *Dyestuffs* case,[9] the Court defined a concerted practice as "a form of co-ordination between undertakings which, without having reached the stage where an agreement properly so-called has been concluded, knowingly substitutes practical co-operation between them for the risks of competition which do not correspond to the normal conditions of the market, having regard to the nature of the products, the importance and number of the undertakings, as well as the size and importance of the said market. Such practical co-operation amounts to a concerted practice". In the second case, *Wood Pulp*[10], the Court ruled that Article 85 does not "deprive economic operators of the right to adapt themselves intelligently to the existing and anticipated conduct of their competitors". More recent

---

[7] The provisions of Art. 85 have been held to apply to vertical agreements since the ECJ's decision in Joined Cases 56 & 58/64 *Etablissements Consten and Grundig* v. *Commission* [1966] ECR 299, [1966] CMLR 418.

[8] See the discussion in R. Whish, *Competition Law* (3rd edn., Butterworths, London, 1993), chap. 7.

[9] Joined Cases 48, 49 & 51–57/69 *ICI* v. *Commission* [1972] ECR 619, [1972] CMLR 557 para. 64.

[10] [1985] OJ L85/1, [1985] 3 CMLR 474; Joined Cases C89/85 etc. *A Ahlström Oy* v. *Commission* [1993] ECR I–1307, [1993] 4 CMLR 407.

game theoretic analyses of oligopolistic competition[11] make the issue abundantly clear: in markets which are continuing over time, there is no reason why firms should not successfully collude tacitly without any communication, merely by acting "intelligently". The attempt to bring this behaviour within the prohibition of Chapter I is not likely to be very productive. The "complex monopoly" provisions of the Fair Trading Act 1973, which have been retained in the reforms, are a much more appropriate vehicle for dealing with this situation. It might be better for the guidelines to acknowledge this from the outset.

The Act introduces a procedure for exemptions which parallels the provisions of Article 85(3), and enables firms to argue for exemption on the basis of beneficial effects which can be shown to flow from a particular agreement or type of agreement. Specifically section 9 in Chapter I refers to an agreement which "contributes to (i) improving production or distribution, (ii) promoting technical or economic progress, while allowing consumers a fair share of the resulting benefit", so long as the agreement is limited to achieving these desirable effects and does not have wider effects on competition between the parties. Exemptions operate at three levels. The first is firm specific, where a firm convinces the Director General that there are net beneficial effects from an agreement might otherwise be prohibited. The second level is block exemptions, such as the exemptions under EU competition policy granted for pure R&D agreements and for pure specialisation agreements.[12] The third level grants parallel exemptions to any already granted as block agreements in Europe: this includes situations which fall within the terms of an existing EU exemption, but are not subject to Article 85 because they do not affect inter-state trade. The Act provides for two procedures with respect to the notification of agreements to the Director General. A firm can ask for informal guidance on whether a particular proposed agreement would infringe the prohibition. Clearance would effectively provide immunity from penalties. But it would be given in confidence without consultation of potentially affected parties, and could not therefore provide contractual certainty. Alternatively the firm can ask for a formal decision, which involves a much more rigorous investigation by the Director General, including an assessment of the market and the concerns of interested parties. The decision will be published.

[11] J. Tirole, Theory of Industrial Organisation (MIT Press, Cambridge, Mass., 1989), chap. 6; L. Phlips, Competition Policy: A Game Theoretic Perspective (CUP, Cambridge, 1995), chaps. 1–3.

[12] Block exemptions for vertical agreements in place under Art. 85(3) include exclusive distribution, exclusive purchasing, franchises, and special arrangements for the retailing of beer, petrol and motor vehicles. See EC Commission, Green Paper on Vertical Restraints in EC Competition Policy COM (96)721 (Brussels, 1997), chap. IV, for a summary. These are not discussed in the Chapter I draft guidelines because of the intention that vertical agreements will be dealt with separately under the Competition Act in a departure from European precedent for Art. 85.

The most significant innovation from the point of view of previous UK competition policy is the provision enabling the Director General to levy fines on firms that are found to be breaking the prohibitions. Once again the legislation follows European precedent in fixing the maximum fine at 10 per cent of UK turnover, recognising that anti-competitive behaviour in the form of cartels can be very profitable and therefore the penalties need to be large to act as a deterrent. The Director General can also require an agreement to be abandoned by the firms involved. The firms have a right of appeal on both the substance and the penalties to a tribunal which will form part of a new body, the Competition Commission. This tribunal will operate entirely independently of government. It will not carry out its own investigations, but rely on the evidence already prepared by the parties.[13] Should the tribunal decide that further evidence is needed it will be able to refer the matter back to the Director General for further consideration at that stage, or ask that the evidence be provided to it. The tribunal will be able to revise both the findings of the Director General and the proposed fine. It will also be open to third parties to appeal to the tribunal if they can show sufficient interest in the case: such third parties may include general consumer organisations. The Act also includes provisions for third party actions for damages or interim relief from the effects of a prohibited agreement. These will be heard in the courts rather than in the tribunal. However a third party will be able to introduce a decision of the Director General or tribunal as evidence that the prohibition has been breached, rather than having to establish the facts anew.

It should be evident that Chapter I of the Act conforms in most respects to the "ideals" for competition policy set out in the first section of this chapter. Although the objectives of the legislation have been described by the government in terms of promoting competition and protecting consumer interests rather than the pursuit of economic efficiency, in this case the two coincide. Promoting competition by preventing price or market-sharing agreements between firms is virtually always consistent with economic efficiency. Furthermore the presumption against agreements is so strong that a general prohibition is the natural starting point, subject to the appreciability test which includes the precedents created by European decisions, and subject to the exclusion of small agreements (except for price fixing). The duty laid on the Director General to publish guidelines is to be welcomed, since it should reduce the costs of compliance by enabling firms to know the situations in which the prohibitions are likely to be applied. The draft guidelines produced by the OFT are generally very sensible. The provisions for exemptions also comply with our

[13] The procedure is likely to involve an appeal, a defence, a reply and a rejoinder, all written submissions. New evidence can be brought into the first two stages e.g. the appellant may wish to provide new evidence in the light of the DGFT's decision from which he is appealing.

model of policy, in that they recognise the possibility of ambiguity in the economic analysis. The system of block exemptions will reduce the administrative costs of the Office of Fair Trading and the compliance costs of firms, while the provision for individual exemptions will enable special cases to be considered on their merits. The institution of fines for infringements, coupled with the possibility of third party actions for damages, gives firms powerful incentives to comply with the prohibition. Finally the harmonisation of this aspect of competition policy with Europe is to be welcomed for the reasons adduced in the first section.

There remains the question whether the new policy instrument is an improvement on what went before. The answer has to be a resounding yes. The previous policy framework attracted many criticisms: the fact that the target of the policy was the form rather than the effects of an agreement, and the lack of penalties for operating cartels, were the criticisms most frequently voiced. The only surprise is that such an imperfect instrument of policy was allowed to last so long, once its defects became apparent.[14] "More like Europe" is an undoubted improvement.

Abuse of a Dominant Position

The core of this part of the Act is section 18. This states in subsection (1) that "any conduct on the part of one or more undertakings which amounts to the abuse of a dominant position is prohibited . . .". Examples of abuse are then given in subsection (2):

"Conduct may, in particular, constitute such an abuse if it consists in—
(a) directly or indirectly imposing unfair purchase or selling prices or other unfair trading conditions;
(b) limiting production, markets or technical development to the prejudice of consumers;
(c) applying dissimilar conditions to equivalent transactions with other trading parties, thereby placing them at a competitive disadvantage;
(d) making the conclusion of contracts subject to acceptance by the other parties of supplementary obligations which, by their nature or according commercial usage, have no connection with the subject of the contracts."

This is, of course, Article 86. The borrowing is deliberate: the policy is meant to parallel precisely European competition law. The institutional framework is essentially that described in the previous section with respect

---

[14] The point should not however be over-emphasised. Early judgments in the Restrictive Practices Court left firms in no doubt that it would be very difficult to satisfy the criteria for exemption laid down in the Act, and the result was a wholesale abandonment of restrictive agreements in the late 1950s and early 1960s. Moreover it would have been relatively easy to amend the legislation to allow the Court to impose fines: the failure of successive governments to do so reflected a reluctance to make the competition policy regime tougher.

to agreements between firms. The Director General of Fair Trading has a duty to investigate suspected abuses, and powers to fine firms up to 10 per cent of UK turnover, to halt the conduct which led to the abuse, and to order the firm to behave in specified ways (e.g. to supply a firm which it had previously refused to supply). The firm has a right of appeal to the Competition Commission tribunal against both the finding of an abuse and the punishment imposed by the Director General. Small and medium sized firms are excluded from the prohibition under the rubric of "conduct of minor significance". A prior screen based on firm market share and/or turnover is to be applied to ensure that the conduct of small firms is not considered. Apart from that, no other exclusions or exemptions are envisaged, apart from mergers and other situations where other competition rules are more relevant. In particular there is no procedure for exemptions along the lines of Article 85(3). The Act requires the Director General to publish guidelines to clarify the way in which he or she proposes to apply the prohibition, and European precedent again applies. As in the case of Chapter I above, a firm may apply for negative guidance on whether a proposed conduct would breach the prohibition. It can ask for informal guidance or for a decision. The former involves a less rigorous analysis, but does not give the same degree of assurance to the firm as the latter, which is given after a full assessment of the matter, including consultation with potentially affected third parties.

Evidently a key feature of policy under Chapter II is the practical definition of "dominant position". The Office of Fair Trading has given thought to this issue in draft guidelines on *Market Definition*. These propose the use of a "hypothetical monopolist test: would a hypothetical monopolist of these products maximise its profits by charging higher prices than it would if it faced competition?" The method begins with a narrow market definition and looks at the substitution possibilities on both the demand side and the supply side in response to a price 5–10 per cent above the competitive level. If a hypothetical monopolist in this narrow market would not be able to raise prices because within a year[15] consumers would switch to other products or new suppliers would enter, then these demand and supply substitutes are added to the market and the test is applied again. In evaluating demand side substitution the Office has indicated that it will use a variety of sources including surveys of customers and competitors, evidence on switching costs, previous price histories of potential substitutes and evidence on price elasticities. Supply-side substitution will be assessed by asking potential suppliers about the feasibility (technical and economic) of supplying the market, including the availability of capacity. Within the UK an important issue is the geographic extent of the relevant markets and the degree to which those markets are effectively open

---

[15] This is a rule of thumb: in the circumstances of particular markets it might be appropriate to consider longer or shorter periods than one year.

to imports from other UK regions or indeed from abroad. Particularly interesting issues arise in the case of products which are intrinsically complementary: for example cars and car parts, or office equipment and servicing. The focus is on the "secondary market": once the customer has bought the first product he may be effectively tied in to the purchase of the second product. The main issue is whether potential customers are sufficiently alert to the costs, not only of the initial purchase, but also the secondary products or services. If they are, then competition in the initial market will be sufficient to prevent the manufacturer trying to exploit captive customers in the secondary market. Having defined the market, it remains to define dominance within that market. The Office notes that the European competition authorities have found businesses to be dominant when they have market shares of 40 per cent, and greater market shares increase substantially the probability that the firm will be identified as dominant. Conversely shares of less than 20–25 per cent are unlikely to be identified as dominant.

Unfortunately, the copying of European policy has brought with it the curious concept of "joint dominance", which arises from the reference to "one or more undertakings" in the wording of section 18 (Article 86). Until the *Italian Flat Glass* case in 1992, the consensus was that this provision was redundant: overt collusive behaviour in oligopoly is caught under Article 85, and tacit collusion under the definition of "concerted practices". Clearly the Commission did not feel that this consensus gave it sufficient leverage on oligopolies, and in *Italian Flat Glass* the Court of First Instance agreed in principle, though not on the facts of the particular case. The judgment is:

> "There is nothing, in principle, to prevent two or more independent economic entities from being, on a specific market, united by such economic links that, by virtue of that fact, together they hold a dominant position vis-à-vis the other operators on the same market."[16]

It would be better for the Office of Fair Trading to issue a self-denying ordinance in respect of this piece of confusion in European policy. The European precedent is a poor one and it would be good to signal that at the beginning of the new regime in the UK. Regrettably, the draft guidelines envisage circumstances in which the Office of Fair Trading might wish to invoke the doctrine, though without detailing what those circumstances might be (paragraph 5.12).

The economic evaluation of "abuse of a dominant position" is much less straightforward than that of anti-competitive agreements. First, it is not entirely evident that all the conduct which Chapter II is attacking is detrimental to economic efficiency. To explore this we need to translate

---

[16] Joined Cases T–68, 77 & 78/89 etc. *Società Italiano Vetro SpA* v. *Commission* [1992] ECR II–1403, [1992] 5 CMLR 302. For further discussion see Whish, n. 8 above, 280–2.

the examples given in section 18 of the Act (Article 86) into the terminology of modern industrial organisation economics. The draft *Guide to the Chapter II Prohibition* issued by the Office of Fair Trading attempts a brief translation (paragraphs 3.1 to 3.5). Clauses (a) and (b) of the section are primarily directed to the classic monopoly, which exploits its market power, either directly by fixing monopoly prices, or indirectly by restricting supplies to the market and benefiting from the resulting higher market price. The interpretation of "imposition of unfair trading conditions" remains unclear as no specific examples are given: the *Guide* states "competition is not always about price alone: quality of products and services and other trading conditions can be significant". The *Guide* also suggests that clause (a) applies to cases of predatory pricing and clause (b) to refusal to supply. Predatory behaviour is not included in the examples of abuse given in section 18 (Article 86), though the section is presumably drafted sufficiently widely to allow the authorities to act where a dominant firm is behaving anti-competitively with respect to existing or potential competitors.

Clause (c) is more problematic. On the face of it, it is referring primarily to price discrimination. The draft *Guide* confirms this interpretation: "dominant firms may be able to charge different prices or impose different conditions on different customers which can allow them to exploit those customers who face least competition without losing customers where competition does exist". An alternative interpretation of (c) is that it is directed at some instances of predatory behaviour, and this interpretation is picked up by the guide: "[i]t can also allow them to target customers who face competition by setting predatory prices in order to drive out competitors". For example a situation in which a dominant firm is experiencing competition in a part of its market, so it cuts price only in that sub-market to drive off the competitor.

Section (d) may also be applied to vertical restraints such as exclusivity agreements, tie-ins and full line forcing, and, as previously noted, section (b) to refusal to supply. The evident difficulties of legislating for the regulation of vertical market relationships have been met by introducing a general provision in Chapter V, to permit the Secretary of State to make Orders for any provision of Chapters I and II to apply in relation to vertical agreements, or for explicit exclusions or exemptions. We comment briefly on this in the next section below.

When the Office of Fair Trading came to drafting guidelines on Chapter II, it very sensibly abandoned the attempt to interpret clauses (a) to (d) directly in terms of economic analysis. Instead it distinguishes:

"conduct which exploits customers of suppliers through, for example: excessively high prices; and discriminatory prices, or other terms and conditions; or

conduct which is anti-competitive, because it will remove or limit competition
from existing competitors, or because it will exclude new undertakings from
entering the market by, for example: 'predatory' behaviour; vertical restraints;
or refusing to supply existing or potential competitors."

Excessively high prices are very obviously inefficient in economic terms—not
only is there a loss in welfare, but there is also the distinct possibility that the
firm will not achieve productive efficiency. However the European precedents
do not inspire much confidence, and in fact there have been very few of
them. The difficulties are illustrated by the *United Brands*[17] case, where the
Court defined the abuse in the following terms: "charging a price which is
excessive because it has no reasonable relation to the economic value of the
product supplied . . . is an abuse". To demonstrate an abuse the Commission
first would have to undertake a cost analysis, and then ask "whether the
difference between the costs actually incurred and the price actually charged
is excessive, and, if the answer to this question is in the affirmative, to
consider whether a price has been charged which is either unfair in itself or
when compared to other competing products". It is scarcely surprising that
the Commission has not often embarked on such an ill defined quest, and
that the draft guidelines suggest that the Office of Fair Trading will similarly
be cautious. The obvious difficulty is to distinguish abusive prices from
prices that are high because of the normal working of the market mecha-
nism. The best the guidelines can do is to point to examples where firms are
able to earn supranormal profits without stimulating new entry.

The verdict of economic analysis on price discrimination is very far from
negative; in many, if not all, situations it is fairly easy to show that it is
actually conducive to economic efficiency. The point is that it generally
extends the market: discrimination is what gives the firm the incentive to
supply into different markets distinguished by buyer, location or time. The
objection to price discrimination can only be sustained as a general proposition if the sole objective is to maximise consumer welfare (and producer
surplus is ignored), or if there are other concerns about equal treatment for
all customers. It is of course entirely reasonable that the authorities should
decide to include these concerns among the objectives of competition
policy—the recurrent phrase "fair trading" is an indication of this broader
concern. But the potential loss of efficiency should be noted. For example,
if there are high fixed costs involved in producing a product, then price
discrimination may be the most efficient way of recouping those costs while
supplying the widest possible market: indeed there may be no single price
which enables the firm to break even, so prohibition of price discrimination
may mean that the product is not supplied at all. In a series of decisions the
European authorities have moved decisively against such discriminatory
practices as loyalty rebates, selective discounting and delivered pricing.

[17] Case 27/76 *United Brands* v. *Commission* [1978] ECR 207, [1978] 1 CMLR 429.

They have been particularly opposed to geographical price discrimination across the markets of the Member States of the European Union, as evidenced by the famous *United Brands* case where the issue was charging different prices for bananas in Eire and Germany!

Much ambiguity is also present in the economic analysis of predatory pricing.[18] In the short term, consumers benefit from low prices, even if in the long term the successful predator can charge higher prices. Moreover it is not easy to distinguish the normal competitive response in a market in which a firm is experiencing competition, from a predatory response which is seeking the demise of the competitor. The key European cases are *AKZO*[19] and *Tetra Pak II*.[20] Both these cases correspond in some degree to the common sense definition of predation, in that in each case a dominant firm moved to counter competition in part of its market by cutting prices. However the problem of defining a predatory price was never resolved satisfactorily beyond a presumption that a price less than average variable cost is predatory. The Court suggested that some evidence of intent to drive out a competitor was required, if prices exceeded average variable cost. This uncertainty as to what would count as predation is very unsatisfactory, and runs the risk of chilling normal price competition in markets with dominant firms.

On vertical restraints the economic analysis is once again ambiguous. If the upstream and downstream markets are sufficiently competitive, the consensus is that competition policy should not concern itself with vertical restraints which simply reflect different marketing strategies adopted by the firms. But where there are dominant firms at either level a degree of caution is appropriate,[21] and these are the situations which Chapter II is designed to catch. For example where there is a dominant firm upstream a vertical agreement may be the means of protecting monopoly power through to the final market, since it precludes the firm from making secret deals with other downstream firms. On one point the analysis is completely clear: there is no basis for treating resale price maintenance (RPM) any differently from other vertical restraints, since other restraints can easily replicate the effects of RPM. The draft guidelines give a full account of the range of vertical restraints that are likely to be of concern, together with the relevant European cases.

The last type of abuse identified in the draft guidelines is refusal to

---

[18] See Phlips, n. 11 above, chap. 4.

[19] Case C–62/86 *AKZO Chemie BV* v. *Commission* [1991] ECR I–3359, [1993] 5 CMLR 215.

[20] Case C–333/94P *Tetra Pak II* [1996] ECR I–5951.

[21] See J. Vickers, "Market power and inefficiency: A Contracts Perspective", 12(4) *Oxford Review of Economic Policy* 11–26; EC Commission n. 12 above, ch. II and P.W. Dobson and M. Waterson, *Vertical Restraints and Competition Policy* (OFT, Research Paper 12, London, 1996).

supply. Here the problem for policy is not so much the economic analysis as the difficulty of distinguishing refusal to supply as an anti-competitive practice and normal commercial decisions. The relevant European cases are the *Commercial Solvents* and *Hugin* cases.[22] In both cases a dominant firm ceased supplies to a firm which was an actual competitor in a downstream market, which the dominant firm was supplying or planning to supply either itself or through a subsidiary. Later decisions of the Commission apparently extended the obligation on a dominant firm to supply even a new entrant. There is a particular concern that dominant firms that have control over a key facility (e.g. a port, a distribution network, a computer network) should not be able to protect a monopoly in services using that facility.

We may now evaluate this area of policy in terms of the propositions of the first section. As already noted the objectives of the policy implicit in Chapter II of the Act and in the draft guidelines must go beyond economic efficiency to include some notions of equality of treatment for customers and "fair competition".[23] Our view is that this introduces a lack of clarity in the analysis of market situations and conduct, and that it runs the risk of inhibiting behaviour which is in fact conducive to economic efficiency.

Whatever one's views on objectives of policy, it is surely essential that a prohibition should be clear about what is prohibited, and in what circumstances. With respect to circumstances, the definition of dominance proposed by the Office of Fair Trading is entirely sensible even if a firm might find it difficult to decide whether it is in fact dominant within a relevant market. The draft guidelines interpreting the prohibitions of section 18 of the Act are also perfectly sensible, but inevitably suffer from the lack of clear definition of what constitutes an "abuse" of a dominant position. Firm behaviour in markets is many dimensional, and there is no agreed definition of what is, or is not, conducive to competition (which is itself undefined). The more the Office can do to exemplify "abuses" in the guidelines, the more effective the policy will be, recalling that the primary objective of policy is to educate firms into the rules of the market game that they must follow, and not to "catch them out".

Given the ambiguity of economic analysis of the efficiency effects of the types of market conduct which are the targets of the legislation, it is disappointing (to an economist, at least) that there is no provision for exemptions along the lines of Chapter I. In its anxiety to mimic Article 86, the legislation has imported a weakness of European policy. It surely would be

---

[22] Respectively Joined Cases 6–7/73 *Commercial Solvents* v. *Commission* [1974] ECR 223, [1974] 1 CMLR 309, and Case 22/78 *Hugin Kassaregister* v. *Commission* [1979] ECR 1869, [1979] 3 CMLR 345.

[23] It would be difficult to justify a *general* prohibition of price discrimination without some such objectives: and at least some of the popular concern about "predation" and price discrimination is a desire to protect the little guy against big business.

sensible to give firms the explicit opportunity to argue on economic efficiency grounds that particular conduct which might otherwise be identified as an abuse has beneficial effects. In practice European policy has tried to come to terms with this need by developing the doctrine of objective justification and the principle of proportionality. In essence these are back-door means of permitting firms to argue that conduct which is *prima facie* an abuse under Article 86 may none the less be deemed innocent if there is an objective justification for it, and if the conduct is no more than is proportionate to protect that justification. However this falls far short of the comprehensive exemption doctrines of Article 85(3): and in practice it has not been used to argue countervailing economic efficiency benefits as an objective justification.

The provisions for the imposition of fines and other conditions on firms which are found to have abused a dominant position are to be welcomed. If the exercise of monopoly power is profitable, then firms have to be given incentives to comply with the rules. The possibility of third party actions to recover damages is also important in giving policy the teeth it previously lacked.

Very evidently Chapter II of the Act brings policy in the UK into line with European policy, and once again the intention is that European experience will be normative for the application of the rules. This harmonisation is to be welcomed, even though we have reservations about the substance of Article 86, and in particular the absence of any procedure for exemption.

Finally there is the question whether the reform represents an improvement on the previous policy in the UK. The legislative framework for the previous policy was the 1980 Competition Act which defined the concept of anti-competitive practice and provided for remedies. Under that policy regime it fell to the Director General to investigate alleged anti-competitive practices, and if adverse effects were identified either to seek undertakings from the firm to desist from the practice or, in more serious cases, to refer the matter to the Monopolies and Mergers Commission.

It is not evident that the switch to a policy modelled on Article 86 is in all respects an improvement. The problem is, as outlined above, that the evaluation of the "abuses" identified by the Act and by the draft guidelines cannot be clear cut. In terms of economic efficiency alone, a general prohibition is simply not supported in the same way that a general prohibition of cartels, for example, is supported. It might nevertheless be argued that a prohibition is the best way to proceed, but *only* if there are provisions for firms to argue for exemption on efficiency grounds. The prohibition would make it clear that competition policy is going to be tough, while the possibility of exemption gives firms an incentive to provide the information on which a more favourable evaluation of a particular practice might be based. It might be argued that the Act does permit conduct to be evaluated

generally since "it is the actual or potential effects of a practice or policy
which will determine whether it is abusive" (*Guide to the Major Provisions
of the Competition Act,* section 5.6), reflecting the wording of the Act
which in section 18 refers to "any conduct . . . which amounts to the abuse
of a dominant position". However this is not the same as an exemption,
since if the effects are those of the abuse of a dominant position, then the
practice should attract condemnation and punishment whatever its
efficiency. The draft *Guide to the Chapter II Prohibition* seeks to soften the
impact of the legislation by adopting the European terminology of "objective justification". Thus section 5.14 states "[i]n general, price discrimination will not be an abuse in such industries [*sc.* Industries with large fixed
costs and low marginal costs e.g. utilities] if it leads to higher levels of
output than an undertaking could achieve by charging every customer the
same price". Similarly in section 5.29, vertical restraints may be objectively
justified if there are countervailing efficiency gains. As already noted, this
is not as useful as an Article 85(3)-type clause with the possibility of block
exemptions. Every case will have to be argued on its individual merits.

The provisions for punishment under the new policy framework are a
definite improvement. Under the old policy regime the Director General or
the Monopolies and Mergers Commission could condemn certain
practices as anti-competitive, but there were no punishments. A firm therefore had every incentive to behave anti-competitively until the practices
were brought to light and the firm was told not to misbehave in future.
After all there was a reasonable chance it might never be found out!

Finally, there is one respect in which the new policy framework definitely
represents a step backwards. Effectively firm conduct is either "not guilty",
or "guilty of an abuse and therefore fined": what is missing is an alternative
finding of "not an abuse but not conducive to competition", with the
imposition of a structural remedy or order to desist from particular
conduct.

Vertical Agreements

As noted above the policy on vertical agreements between firms at different
levels of the supply chain to final consumers is still undefined. The original
intention was that vertical agreements should be excluded from the
category of anti-competitive agreements prohibited in Chapter I, but it
proved difficult to produce a satisfactory draft to achieve this without
unintentionally excluding some potentially anti-competitive agreements
between competitors. The issue is now addressed by section 50, which
simply permits the Secretary of State "by order [to] provide for any provision [of the Act] to apply in relation to . . . vertical agreements", and goes
on to state that "vertical agreements" may have such meaning as prescribed

by an order. The Office of Fair Trading has promised draft guidelines on the subject, but these have not yet appeared.[24]

Leaving aside the legislative and administrative difficulties, we may concentrate on the relevant competition issues. As already noted the consensus of economic analysis is that vertical agreements become a problem *only if competition is absent* in either the upstream or downstream market.[25] The European *Green Paper on Vertical Restraints in EC Competition Policy* summarises the conclusions as follows: "[t]he fiercer is interbrand competition the more likely are the pro-competitive and efficiency effects to outweigh any anti-competitive effects of vertical restraints. The inverse is true when interbrand competition is weak and there are significant barriers to entry." The basic idea is that vertical restraints create vertical structures of firms and distributors, including retailers, which compete in markets. If the markets are competitive, then there are efficiency gains from vertical restraints: vertical co-ordination in pricing to avoid "double marginalisation", and co-ordination in the provision of services to overcome incentive and free-rider problems. Vertical agreements may also be important for solving risk-sharing and moral hazard problems between the upstream and downstream firms without introducing efficiency losses.

But if competition is absent, then there are grounds for competition policy. Lack of competition could arise either through a collusive agreement or due to a dominant firm. In the first case, the policy should aim to prevent firms from entering into *horizontal* agreements to introduce vertical restraints for their downstream buyers: the case of manufacturing firms jointly imposing resale price maintenance or territorial restrictions on their retailers comes naturally to mind. The reasoning is that joint imposition of such vertical restraints might help to maintain cartel discipline, or to make the market much less competitive. In the second case, a dominant firm might wish to impose vertical restraints in order to prevent downstream competition among its retailers dissipating monopoly rents, to tie its own hands not to make secret deals with selected retailers which would also undermine its profits, or to make it more difficult for a potential rival to enter (foreclosure). Effectively the policy should aim to prohibit firms from making horizontal agreements to impose vertical restraints on their retailers (subject of course to a *de minimis* provision), should identify vertical restraints as potential abuses by dominant firms, and in both cases should make provision for exemptions.

European policy has proceeded by making use of exemptions from Article 85, which does not distinguish vertical and horizontal, and therefore captures the whole range of vertical agreements. In particular, block exemptions have been issued for exclusive distribution agreements (Regulation

---

[24] As at Sept. 1998.
[25] See n. 21 above.

1983/83), exclusive purchasing (Regulation 1984/83) with special rules for beer and petrol distribution, and franchising (Regulation 4087/88). There is no parallel block exemption for selective distribution systems, though there is now a substantial body of cases which indicate what will and will not be allowed under individual exemptions, and there is a special regime for motor vehicle distribution and servicing agreements (Regulation 123/84). However dominant firms (in the terms of Article 86) cannot rely on these exemptions. For example in *BPB Industries plc* v. *Commission* and *Hoffmann-La Roche* v. *Commission*[26] exclusive purchasing agreements were condemned where the supplier was a dominant firm. However there have not been many cases in which the issue has been tested by the Commission or before the European Court.

Since there was no means of drafting Chapter I to exclude vertical agreements, the Orders under section 50 of the Act will have to incorporate something akin to these European exemption regulations under Article 85(3).[27] But care will have to be taken to ensure that agreements between upstream firms to impose vertical restraints on downstream firms are not unintentionally exempted. It would be good to make it absolutely clear that any exemptions do not apply to dominant firms, whose conduct will continue to be scrutinised under Chapter II. The absence of an exemption procedure in Chapter II is a serious lack, as the ambiguity of the economic analysis is perhaps greater here than in any other single competition policy issue. The Office of Fair Trading guidelines, when they appear, should do everything to infiltrate a rule of reason approach, under the guise of the "objective justification" doctrine.

Scale Monopolies, Complex Monopolies and Mergers

As already noted an important feature of the new competition policy framework is the retention of so-called "structural" policies to deal with scale monopolies, complex monopolies and mergers. The first two of these have no parallels in European policy: the third is an area where European policy was relatively undeveloped until the Merger Regulation (4064/89) was introduced in 1989. In the UK all three areas are dealt with under the Fair Trading Act 1973, and follow similar procedures. The market situation or merger is investigated first by the Office of Fair Trading (in conjunction with the Mergers Panel in the case of mergers), and if the

[26] Case T–65/89 *BPB Industries plc* v. *Commission* [1993] ECR II–389 and Case 85/76 *Hoffmann-La Roche* v. *Commission* [1979] ECR 461, [1979] 3 CMLR 211.

[27] But probably not the special exemptions for beer, petrol and motor vehicle distribution and servicing which should be scrutinised carefully for their suitability in the UK domestic market.

Director General believes that there should be a full investigation he advises the Secretary of State to refer the matter to the Monopolies and Mergers Commission.

In cases of scale monopoly or complex monopoly the first task of the Commission is to ascertain that a 25 per cent market share criterion is fulfilled. A "monopoly" is where a single firm has more than 25 per cent of the market or markets which are the subject of the reference. A "complex monopoly" is basically a group of firms which has a joint 25 per cent share,[28] where the firms involved are behaving similarly even though there is no evidence of an agreement between them. In a merger case the criterion is again a 25 per cent market share, or a test based on the value of assets involved in the merger. Evidently this raises the same issues of market definition discussed above.

The MMC investigation is guided by a criterion of the public interest, defined to include effective competition, consumer interests, innovation, balanced regional distribution of industry and employment, and the international competitive position of UK producers. The MMC reports to the Secretary of State, giving its findings in respect of the matters referred and making recommendations if the market situation or merger is found to be contrary to the public interest. Recommendations can include seeking undertakings from a monopolist or oligopoly in respect of business practices, the implementation of price control, and even structural changes such as divestment: in the case of a merger the recommendation can be that the merger be disallowed or that it should be made subject to conditions. There are no penalties for past anti-competitive behaviour. It is for the Secretary of State to decide whether to approve or vary the remedies (if any) recommended in the MMC report. All these policy provisions are to be carried forward, essentially unchanged, into the new competition policy framework. The MMC will become the Competition Commission in its reporting mode, and nothing else will change.

The first point to make about this policy in respect of scale monopolies and complex monopolies is that the retention of the provisions of the Fair Trading Act 1973 is a definite gain in comparison with European policy. Economic analysis has long recognised that there are market structures and practices which can result in loss of competition and economic efficiency without any obvious abuse of a dominant position by the firm or group of firms involved. In such cases the obvious remedies are structural, or, if that is too difficult to achieve, some degree of regulation (as in the case of the privatised utilities which are also natural monopolies). Being 'unlike Europe' in this area of competition policy is a good thing.

---

[28] It is natural to think of oligopolies, but parallel behaviour by a large number of small firms could also be investigated if their combined market share was 25%, as in the MMC medical services case.

One oddity about the new regime is that a reference of a scale monopoly to the Competition Commission can only be made in future if the firm in question has already been found to have abused a dominant position in a market and has been fined. This introduces an unnecessary complication. Either it is appropriate to deal with an abuse by a fine and an order under Chapter II, which should surely be an adequate deterrent to anti-competitive behaviour, or if there is a structural problem without any identifiable abuse of dominance ask for an investigation by the Commission. It would therefore be logical to leave the two approaches as distinct options open to the Director General (as they are for the utility regulators under the new regime), perhaps with the proviso that a firm could not be called to account under both options at the same time.

Another oddity is that the policy framework has retained the MMC in the form of the reporting function of the Competition Commission to undertake this work. One wonders why the procedures have not been changed to bring them into line with the procedures proposed for Chapters I and II cases. That is, a system where the initial investigation is undertaken by the Office of Fair Trading, presumably by experienced staff reassigned from the current MMC. The Director General would then issue a report and assessment, including any action that should be taken, such as refusing a merger, requiring a dominant firm to desist from certain market practices, or even some structural changes (e.g. divestment). There would then be a right of appeal to the Competition Commission, as in Chapter I and II cases. This system would remove the role of the Secretary of State in receiving and deciding upon recommendations from the reporting arm of the Competition Commission. If the objective of policy is to promote competition then it is hard to see any justification for involvement of ministers in implementation, which should be purely administrative. The argument against similar procedures for all competition cases[29] is that there will be a significant difference in "culture" between cases under Chapters I and II, and the wider ranging enquiries in structural cases. The concern is that the inevitably legalistic approach of the former would spread to the latter.

We now turn to the evaluation of this area of policy in terms of the criteria set out in the first section of the chapter. The public interest criterion has been retained despite considerable criticism: and the assurance that references to the Commission will be made primarily on competition grounds is only partly reassuring. It just seems odd to have competition as the basis for the Chapter I and Chapter II policy, and then have something different for structural policy. There is no point of principle which would

[29] Apart from the adage "if it ain't broke, don't fix it" (attributed to Bert Lance, an American government official, in *The Nation's Business*, May 1977): after all the present MMC system appears to be working well enough. Moreover the current reforms have the undoubted advantage of legislative simplicity for the government.

support the divergence. (And, of course, an economist would prefer the criterion to be economic efficiency.[30])

In respect of rules, the essence of structural policies is that there is no presumption as to the effect of structure on competition, so prohibitions are not relevant. So a full investigation of particular cases is in order. However there is much to be said for the development of guidelines, perhaps along the lines of the US Department of Justice Merger Guidelines, and especially if this were linked to changing the burden of proof (on this more below).

We have already noted that structural policies are missing from European competition policy, except for mergers. So the issue of harmonisation of policy does not arise. On mergers there are no fundamental differences of approach: in particular there is no presumption for or against merger, and each case is addressed on its merits.

Finally we consider briefly an aspect of competition policy which is neglected by both the European and UK policy regimes. If one is concerned about competition (either for its own sake or as a means to economic efficiency), then there is much to be said for a policy which aims to prevent potentially anti-competitive market situations emerging. The antitrust legislation of the United States in section 2 of the Sherman Act 1890 recognises this in measures to prevent "attempting to monopolize a market". In principle dominant positions in markets can arise in a number of different circumstances. The first is public grant as in the privatisation of utilities in the UK in recent years. A government which is serious about competition should ensure that the market structure created by privatisation is as competitive as possible, given the circumstances of the industry. Where competition is not possible, as in the case of natural monopolies, then some regulatory framework will have to be put in place from the beginning. The 1998 Act strengthens the hand of the regulators by bringing the regulated utilities within its scope. In particular, regulators will now be able to apply Chapter II to counter any abuse of a dominant position, including the power to impose a fine for anti-competitive behaviour.

The second route to market dominance is "skill, foresight and industry". This is when a firm has competed vigorously and successfully in terms of products, quality and price, and has seen off the competition in the process. This is the defence that has been advanced in a number of recent

---

[30] It can be argued that in practice the public interest criterion will continue to be interpreted by the first three criteria of S. 84 of the Fair Trade Act, which are competition, consumer benefit and innovation: the last two criteria (exports and regional employment) having hardly ever been used. In which case there is no substantive difference from Chaps. I and II. However in the past there have been cases where matters that have no connection to competition have been considered—e.g. the MMC reports on Lonrho/House of Fraser (1979) or EldersIXL/Allied Lyons (1986)—and there is no guarantee that such cases will not occur in future if the public interest criterion is retained.

antitrust cases in high technology sectors: it was argued by IBM in the 1970s and will no doubt be argued by Microsoft. The concern is, of course, that such firms having achieved dominance by acceptable means may resort to anti-competitive actions to preserve that dominance, and that they may abuse their dominant position by charging monopoly prices. It would not be sensible to try to stop firms achieving dominance by this route: but once they have achieved it there is every reason for the competition authorities to keep a very close eye on their continuing activities to prevent abuse (under Article 86 or Chapter II).

The third route is by anti-competitive market practices. The focus here is on predation and vertical restraints. Under the UK framework for policy such behaviour cannot be contested by the competition authorities unless the firm is *already* dominant in the relevant market. However it is not difficult to envisage circumstances in which a multidivisional firm has a relatively small market share in one of the markets in which it operates, but is able to use resources from other divisions to conduct a predatory campaign to gain market share in that market.[31] Once it has passed the threshold for market dominance it may then modify its behaviour to avoid being attacked under the provisions of Chapter II. One way of dealing with this possibility would be to allow the provisions of Chapter II to be applied to the conduct of very large firms (defined on an asset basis, as in the merger policy) even if in the particular market in question the firm is not dominant (yet).

The final route is that of mergers and acquisitions. In principle this route to dominance is well covered by the provisions of current policy. But it would perhaps be wise to consider again the burden of proof in assessing the public interest in mergers *which will potentially create dominant positions*. If the objective of policy, as reiterated by the Government, is to maintain competitive markets, then it surely should be a privilege to be permitted to build a dominant position in a market by merger, and a privilege which should be granted only after the firm has shown net public benefits therefrom.[32] After all mergers are the ultimate "collusive agreements", and such agreements are rigorously opposed under Chapter I. There is a distinct possibility that a tougher policy regime in respect of horizontal agreements will simply increase the incentives for merger. Reversing the burden of proof (in cases where the *de minimis* rules do not apply) would also assist in arriving at an accurate evaluation of a proposed merger, since the firms involved would have every incentive to provide the evidence that the competition authorities required.

---

[31] This point has been persuasively argued by C. Newton in a perceptive comment on the Act: "Do Predators Need to be Dominant?", Competition and Regulation Bulletin (9 July 1998), (London School of Economics, London, 1998).

[32] The argument that the authorities should not interfere in the takeover market, because shareholders know best, is besides the point. Shareholders should indeed support takeovers which create market power for their companies, but that is clearly not in the public interest!

Conclusions

The long awaited reform of competition policy has at last come to fruition in the Competition Act 1998, in the form of a complete incorporation of Articles 85 and 86 in UK legislation. In respect of Chapter I (Article 85) our evaluation is uniformly positive. The Chapter passes all our tests with respect to the objective of policy, the design of policy rules and their implementation (including fines for breaches of the rules), and harmonisation with Europe. In respect of Chapter II (Article 86), we are less enthusiastic. It is far from evident that all of the behaviour prohibited in Chapter II is in fact detrimental to economic efficiency, though there may be other objections (e.g. that price discrimination is not "fair" in some sense). The major weakness, inherited from Article 86, is that there is no scope for a firm to argue for exemption, for example on the basis of economic efficiency. Nor is there provision for an alternative verdict of 'not conducive to competition', followed by a structural remedy or a requirement to desist from a particular market practice. The treatment of vertical issues remains in some doubt, though resale price maintenance continues to receive separate (and harsher) treatment than other vertical restraints, for which there is no justification in industrial economic analysis. There are however some definite gains, such as the guidelines for market definition, the power to fine offenders, and the application of the Chapter to the regulated utilities. The decision to retain those parts of existing competition policy which address scale monopolies, complex monopolies and mergers is to be welcomed. There has not however been any effort to reform the procedures to bring them into line with those for Chapters I and II, and the burden of proof in merger cases remains unchanged. Overall competition policy in the UK after the Competition Act is definitely "more like Europe", and on the whole it is a change for the better, at least in principle.

5

The Competition Act: Some Foreseeable Problems

VALENTINE KORAH*

Exemption Orders, Vertical Restraints

My first heading, exemption orders and vertical restraints, can be very short. The Secretary of State has not yet exercised the power under section 60 to exempt any or all vertical agreements, and the DGFT is delaying consultation and preparation of guidelines meanwhile. It is contemplated that all vertical restraints may be exempted.

All I shall say on this topic is that the distinction between horizontal and vertical agreements drawn in paragraph 1.5 of the OFT's draft guideline[1] on *the Chapter I Prohibition* is unsatisfactory:

> "This guideline is concerned only with horizontal agreements—that is, between undertakings which operate at the same level of the production and distribution chain: the Government has said that it believes that, in general, the majority of vertical agreements—those between undertakings operating in different levels of the chain—do not raise competition concerns."

Suppose that you and I make and supply widgets, but that your technology is so superior to mine that I do not constrain your pricing policy. Suppose, further, that your technology is protected by such a broad patent that I am unlikely to be able to invent around it. Would a licence of that technology to me be horizontal? We are both operating in the production and supply of widgets, but without the licence I could not constrain your market

---

* Professor Emeritus of Competition Law at University College London, visiting professor, College of Europe at Bruges, Fordham University School of Law, the University of Lund and the University of Valencia, Barrister and author. I have written a longer paper on joint dominance and predation for the *Liber Amicorum Michel Waelbroeck*, to be published by Bruylant, I hope early in 1999. I am grateful for constructive criticism of that paper from many people, especially from Bill Bishop and Alison Oldale at Lexicon, the economic consultants. I also enjoyed the competition memo by that firm on "Meeting Competition", 22 June.
[1] Of July 1998.

decisions. According to the US *Antitrust Guidelines for the Licensing of Intellectual Property*,[2] the agreement would be vertical:

> "For analytical purposes, the Agencies ordinarily will treat a relationship between a licensor and its licensees, or between licensees, as horizontal when they would have been actual or likely potential competitors in a relevant market in the absence of the license."

This distinction, based on existing and potential competition, reflects the reasons of policy for treating agreements between competitors and potential competitors more strictly.[3] I hope the UK guidelines may be changed. Marginal problems remain under the US test: how certain and strong must the potential competition be for the agreement to be horizontal?

Collective Dominance

Conduct in Concentrated Markets

The problems of concentrated markets are not well discussed in the OFT guidelines on either the Chapter 1 or Chapter 2 prohibition. Where there are only a few suppliers in a market,[4] it is widely accepted that prices are likely to be higher than they would be were the market less concentrated, and less will be supplied. A realises that if it reduces its prices in the hope of using more of its spare capacity, its competitors will soon notice, as they will lose sales and are likely to reduce their prices too. Consequently A will do so only if it thinks that lower prices by everyone are in its interest.

Similar arguments apply if A is thinking of raising its price. The others know that unless each of them raises its prices fast, A will have to abrogate the increase, so they will not increase their share of the market by not following the initial rise. They are likely to raise their prices on the same range of products and by the same amount within a day or two, unless they think that demand is so responsive to price that lower prices charged

---

[2] 6 April 1995, 3.3, example 5.

[3] Even horizontal agreements may be legal according to the rule of reason in the USA. Some cross-licensing or patent pools enable all the firms to compete unconstrained by blocking patents. On the other hand, if potential competitors are excluded, the cross licences may raise entry barriers. Newcomers will be able to join only if their individual contributions are commensurate with the total value of all the existing members. The issue is not one of the form of the agreement, nor does the answer depend on whether the firms currently compete at the same level of a particular production or distribution chain, but of analysing all the likely effects on the market.

[4] The same problem occurs in the converse case where there are only a few buyers in a market, often undertakings granted special or exclusive rights by the government. The UK had a case on *Mining Ropes* which were bought only by the National Coal Board. With the continued privatisation of nationalised industries, this is becoming a rarer problem than it was.

by everyone would be more profitable. Suppliers are unlikely to compete in ways that can easily and quickly be copied. Price competition will take the form of secret discounts to important buyers who negotiate effectively and are trusted not disclose the low prices they obtain.

While economists regret this, to prohibit A from raising its price or B and C from following it precisely shortly afterwards would be silly policy-wise. It would become impossible for the suppliers to raise their prices as costs rise as an announcement to the customers of each would soon be known to the other suppliers. Each would have to exit the market as its plant required replacement. Out of the frying pan into the fire!

The UK Monopolies Commission in its report on *Parallel Pricing*[5] concluded that the task of remedying the detriments was far from easy since the behaviour results mainly from the structure of the markets in which they operate. It recommended that attention be focused on reducing the number of industries that are concentrated and to introducing pressure for more active competition.

Sometimes entry barriers are created by a licensing requirement imposed by government, or the exclusive rights of nationalised industries. These have been substantially reduced in the UK over the Thatcher years. Mergers making markets more concentrated can be controlled under the Fair Trading Act, and those provisions are to remain in force.

The other sensible remedies introducing pressure for more active competition are restricting unilateral action by oligopolists that makes it easer not to compete with each other or which excludes others. One example of facilitating devices that make it easier for existing firms not to compete with each other is rapidly exchanging sensitive market information such as individual discounts granted, amount of capacity used, unused, to be built or scrapped. Information agreements can, however, be forbidden under Chapter I. The reciprocal exchange of information without prior commitment being established probably amounts to a concerted practice caught by Chapter I.

A unilateral facilitating device that is probably not caught by Chapter I[6] is for the suppliers each to promise most of their large customers "most favoured customer terms". At first sight this seems to enable smaller firms to benefit from the tough negotiation by their larger competitors, but the initial grant of discounts which would have to be widely extended[7] may be

---

[5] Report on the General Effect on the Public Interest of the Practice of Parallel Pricing, July 1973, Cmnd. 5330, paragraph 108.

[6] Compare the Technology Transfer Regulation 240/96, Art. 2(1)(10) and recital 18 which states that a most favoured licensee clause is unlikely to infringe Art. 85(1), but is exempted just in case it may do so.

[7] Of course, the firms may cheat on their other customers by keeping some of the special discounts secret, but if discounts are widespread it is likely to become known to other customers who have reason to care.

discouraged. Secret discounts are often the only price competition possible in concentrated markets.

Announcing price rises well in advance of implementing them has several desirable consequences. The announcement enables customers to make contracts selling their final product in the knowledge of their likely costs; it may enable the seller to clear a glut, and it gives time for the many negotiations that become necessary when basic prices change. On the other hand, it gives time for the suppliers to decide how to react to each price announcement and reduces the risk of the initial price rise since it can be abrogated before it is implemented if others do not follow.[8]

EC Precedents—the Need for Links

Where entry barriers have been imposed by exclusive licences granted by governmental measures, the European Court of Justice (hereafter called "the ECJ") has been interventionist under Article 90 in combination with Article 86.[9] The Commission, confirmed by the Community courts, has frequently condemned exclusionary conduct adopted by a single firm. It would be helpful to condemn unilateral conduct making it easier for oligopolists not to compete with each other or exclude others otherwise than by competition on the merits. For this purpose the Commission has quite frequently objected to the abuse of a jointly held dominant position where there are economic or structural links between them.

The need to use a concept of collective dominance under UK law is less acute than under Article 86, since we will retain power to refer a complex monopoly situation to the Monopolies and Mergers Commission ("MMC"), but the need for links is not entirely academic even in the UK. If unilateral anti-competitive practices are forbidden under Chapter II as construed in conformity with Article 86, it will be illegal for firms to adopt them and there will be no need to make use of the complex monopoly provisions to investigate specific markets. The courts and OFT will be able

---

[8] In Joined Cases 48, 49 & 51–57/69 ICI v. Commission (Dyestuffs) [1972] ECR 619, [1972] CMLR 557, the ECJ focused on the progressive co-ordination of the suppliers who originally followed the price rise announced by one of them within a day or two, but the next rise was announced over two months in advance of implementation and the third was influenced by discussions at a meeting.

[9] E.g., Case C–260/89 ERT [1991] ECR I–2925, [1994] CMLR 540, [1993] 2 CEC 115; Case C–41/90 Höfner and Elser v. Macrotron GmbH [1991] ECR I–1979, [1993] 4 CMLR 306, [1993] 1 CEC 238; Case C–179/90 Merci Convenzionali Porto di Genova v. Siderurgica Gabrielli [1991] ECR I–5889, [1994] 4 CMLR 422. The original initiative to use Art. 90 in combination with Art. 86 came from the Commission when, under Art. 90(3), it adopted the Terminal Equipment Directive for telephones, which was largely confirmed by the ECJ in Case C–202/88 France v. Commission [1991] ECR I–1223, [1992] 5 CMLR 552, [1993] 1 CEC 748.

to enforce the prohibition. I shall, therefore, try to analyse the EC position.

The early judgments of the ECJ were hostile to the concept of collective dominance. In *Vitamins*[10] the Court firmly distinguished oligopolistic inter-dependence from single-firm dominance. Article 86 was not concerned with the former. Roche was found dominant over the supply of vitamin A, a market described by the ECJ as oligopolistic (paragraphs 50–52), but the Commission did not even allege that the producers with smaller market shares were collectively dominant.

In *Ahmed Saeed*,[11] the ECJ did not address the possibility of a collective dominant position when the only two airlines licensed to fly a particular route agreed on fares said to be excessive, but it considered that the exercise by one air carrier of its power to overcharge customers or to exclude rivals by charging unfair prices and forcing the other carrier to do the same might be abusive.

Despite the clear words in *Vitamins*, more recent judgments of both the ECJ and CFI have accepted a concept of joint or collective dominance under Article 86 provided that economic links between the undertakings are established. They have not indicated any policy reasons for requiring economic links before joint dominance is found, nor have they explained what is meant by a link in this context. Does inter-dependent market behaviour in a concentrated market amount to a link?

The relevance of links before collective dominance can be established was first suggested in *Italian Flat Glass*,[12] where the Commission alleged collective dominance when there was no need: when it had forbidden the same co-ordinated conduct under Article 85 and imposed fines of nearly 10 million ecus. On appeal, the CFI accepted a concept of collective dominance where there were economic links between the firms, and it instanced use of the same technology through a technology licence (paragraph 358), but it quashed the part of the Commission's decision on Article 86, as it had merely recycled the facts from which it found an infringement of Article 85.

In *Almelo*,[13] the ECJ strengthened the requirement of a link by treating it as necessary to the establishment of collective dominance and not only as an example. It cited *Bodson* v. *Pompes Funèbres des Régions Libérées SA*,[14] although in *Bodson* the ECJ had not referred to the need for an economic link.

In two later judgments, *Centro Servizi Sporto* v. *Spedizioni Maritima del*

---

[10] Case 85/76 *Hoffmann-La Roche & Co. AG* v. *Commission* [1979] ECR 461, [1979] 3 CMLR 211, CMR 8527, paragraph 39.

[11] Case 66/86 *Ahmed Saeed Flugreisen and Silver Line Reisebüro GmbH* v. *Zentrale zur Bekämpfung Unlauteren Wettbewerbs* [1989] ECR 803, [1990] 4 CMLR 102, [1989] 2 CEC 654, paras. 37–46.

[12] *Fabbrica Pisana SpA and Others* (89/93/EEC), 7 Dec. 1988, [1989] OJ L33/44, [1990] 4 CMLR 535, [1989] 1 CEC 2077; on appeal, Joined Cases T–68, 77 & 78/89 *Società Italiana Vetro SpA* v. *Commission* [1992] ECR II–1403, [1992] 5 CMLR 302, [1992] 2 CEC 33.

[13] Case C–393/92 [1994] ECR I–1477, paras. 41 and 42.

[14] Case 30/87 [1988] ECR 2479, [1989] 4 CMLR 984, [1990] 1 CEC 3, paras. 26–29.

Golfo,[15] (33) and *DIP SpA* v. *Commune di Bassano del Grappa and Comune di Chioggia*,[16] the Court merely referred to *Almelo* and repeated that links were necessary before collective dominance could be established without giving any reasons. It seems that in neither case were there sufficiently few suppliers licensed to amount to an oligopoly so the issue did not arise.

Italian Flat Glass and the later cases were cited in *Compagnie Maritime Belge*.[17] The Court of First Instance stated at paragraph 60 that it is:

"settled case law . . . that Article 86 is capable of applying to situations in which several undertakings together hold a dominant position on the relevant market."

It added that this is true only where links are established.

There clearly were collusive links in *Italian Flat Glass* and *Compagnie Maritime Belge* so the need to establish links was not relevant. There appears to have been no likelihood of parallel pricing in *Centro Servizi Sporto* or in *DIP* where many firms were affected. So consistant case law has been established only by *Almelo*, where an irrelevant judgment was cited for the proposition that joint dominance can be established only where there are links. None of the judgments articulated any policy behind the need for links. The need may make it difficult for the ECJ to fill the gap in the Treaty: the lack of control over unilateral facilitating devices and exclusionary practices by oligopolists.

It is not clear what is meant by the word "links". Clearly it includes the cartel agreement that had been condemned by the Commission in *Cewal* or the technology licensing suggested by the CFI in *Italian Flat Glass*. It might well include a concerted practice operating as a cartel, although it is unlikely that the application of Article 86 would be vital when Article 85 normally applies. Control over a wholly owned subsidiary is not relevant, since a dependent subsidiary would be part of the same undertaking as the parent and the group could be fined as a single undertaking.[18]

---

[15] Case C–96/94 [1995] ECR I–2883, [1996] 4 CMLR 613, para. 33.

[16] Joined Cases C–140 – 142/94 [1995] ECR 1 3257, [1996] 4 CMLR 157.

[17] [1997] OJ L258/1, [1997] 5 CMLR 666.

[18] There might be less than full shareholder or management control, and it is not clear whether the judgment in Case T–102/92 *Viho* v. *Commission* [1995] ECR II–17, [1997] 4 CMLR 469, [1995] CEC 562—on appeal, Case C–73/95P [1996] ECR I–5457, [1997] 4 CMLR 419, would apply where the subsidiary is less than 100 per cent owned. The links through nominated directors might suffice. In *Irish Sugar*, [1997] OJ L258/1, [1997] 5 CMLR 666 [1997] CEC 2380, paras. 111 and 112, the Commission found that Irish Sugar and SDL were jointly dominant, but did not allege that Irish Sugar was the same undertaking as SDL and its parent company, SDH, although Irish Sugar paid for customer promotions and rebates granted by SDL to its customers. It might have argued that since SDL was following the policy determined by Irish Sugar, they should have been treated as a single undertaking, just as the acts of ICI were imputed to Commercial Solvents in Joined Cases 6 & 7/73 *Istituto Chemioterapico Italiano SpA and Commercial Solvents Corp.* v. *Commission* [1974] ECR 223, [1974] 1 CMLR 309, CMR 8209.

Since the lecture was delivered, Advocate General Fennelly considered what might amount to an economic link leading to a single entity in Compagnie Maritime Belge, C–396/96P, October 29, paras. 27–35.

Can one go as far as to suggest that where there are few suppliers, each avidly watching the conduct of its competitors but not colluding, there are "links" of inter-dependence between them?[19]

The need for the concept of collective dominance is to compensate for the Commission's inability to challenge under Article 85 or 86 unilateral conduct that deters entry or makes it easier for the incumbents not to compete with each other. The concept of collective dominance may also be useful, as it was in *Compagnie Maritime Belge*, to reach cartel behaviour which would otherwise come within a group exemption. The concept is needed even more for merger control under EC, but not UK, law. Efforts to apply it may have been frustrated by the Community courts' stress on the need for links between the firms if they are to be found to enjoy a collective dominant position.

It is doubtful whether collective dominance can be established without links between the firms. The issue may not be addressed on the appeal in *Compagnie Maritime Belge*, as there were links in that case. Unless inter-dependent pricing amounts to a link, many concentrations and the anti-competitive behaviour of firms in concentrated markets may be beyond the reach of Community competition law.

If the ECJ cannot be persuaded to expand the concept of a link to include parallel conduct, it may be argued that each of the oligopolists is individually dominant as long as the others do not compete in ways that can be rapidly copied. Each oligopolist may not have a very large market share, but as long as the others do not compete, for instance on list prices, each may have a significant discretion over the prices it can set and its other commercial decisions. This might bring it within the definitions of a dominant position habitually given by the ECJ,[20] but there is no case law to support this view.

I am not suggesting that consciously parallel conduct should amount to an abuse of a dominant position: only that it might lead to a dominant position, the abuse of which might consist of facilitating devices and exclusionary conduct adopted unilaterally. Because of the doubts remaining

---

[19] See Joined Cases C–68/94 & 30/95 *France* v. *Commission* [1998] ECR I–1375, [1998] 4 CMLR 829, para 221, analysed below.

[20] See, for instance, Case 85/76 *Hoffmann-La Roche & Co. AG* v. *Commission (Vitamins)* [1979] ECR 461, [1979] 3 CMLR 211, CMR 8527,

"38. The dominant position thus referred to relates to a position of economic strength enjoyed by an undertaking which enables it to prevent effective competition being maintained on the relevant market by affording it the power to behave to an appreciable extent independently of its competitors, its customers and ultimately of the consumers."

This definition has been used in judgment after judgment. The judgment in *DIP*, cited in note 17 above, paras. 24–28, following para. 64 of the Opinion of Fennelly AG said that it all depended on direct evidence. It seems that it had not beenestablished that the many kinds of traders protected by the licensing requirement under Italian law would be jointly dominant even if there were sufficient links.

about the use of the concept of collective dominance, the UK has decided to retain its power to refer complex monopoly situations to the MMC. Those provisions cannot be used to forbid facilitating or exclusionary devices *ex ante*. Where a market is concentrated, the supply of those products: the complex monopoly situation or steps taken to obtain or maintain it, may be referred to the MMC. Only after the MMC has condemned at least some aspect of the situation or conduct can a restraining order be made.

Oligopolistic Dominance under the Merger Regulation

The UK is not dependent on a notion of joint dominance for merger control. The power to refer mergers to the Monopolies and Mergers Commission is to be retained and a merger need result in a market share of only 25 per cent to be capable of being referred. The EC law relating to "oligopolistic dominance" under the Merger Regulation is relevant under UK law only to the extent that it can be applied also to Article 86.

There is a gap in the EC merger control law: only a merger that creates or strengthens a dominant position as a result of which competition may be significantly impeded can be forbidden. The Commission has been imposing conditions on firms whose mergers are likely to result in "oligopolistic dominance".

In March 1998, in *France v. Commission*, the ECJ concluded that "collective dominant positions do not fall outside the scope of the merger regulation" (paragraph 178) where, owing to "correlative factors", the parties are able to adopt a common policy on the market and act independently of their competitors (paragraph 221). It quashed the Commission's appraisal, however, as it had not established the links that it had alleged. The Commission had not argued that a market structure leading to parallel pricing amounted to a sufficient link.

What are "correlative factors"? Are they relevant also under Article 86? Are they looser than "links"? Does parallel conduct amount to a common policy? Perhaps the Court was adopting a compromise formula that leaves open the possibility that oligopolistic inter-dependence could constitute a sufficient link. The correlative factors are not an exhaustive test, as the ECJ says, "in particular". This opens the argument that either correlative factors or inter-dependent conduct may lead to collective dominance. Does this argument apply under Article 86 or only under the Merger Regulation?

The Court held that a market share outside Germany between the duopolists of 23 per cent and 37 per cent, did not conclusively indicate a collective dominant position (paragraph 226). Although a dominant position is presumed for a single firm at 50 per cent,[21] oligopolists are

---

[21] Case 62/86 *AKZO Chemie BV* v. *Commission* [1991] ECR I–3359, [1993] 5 CMLR 215, [1993] 2 CEC 115, para. 60.

subject to uncertainty over whether competitors will continue not to compete aggressively. So the ECJ may be right to decide that a higher market share is required to establish collective dominance.

Abuse

Predation and Meeting Competition

The OFT's draft *Guide to the Abuse of a Dominant Position Provisions of the Competition Act 1998* [22] states that the distinction between predation and price competition is difficult to draw, but it does not refer to the tension between encouraging the initial investment that led to the incumbent being the only supplier and discouraging new entry otherwise than on the basis of performance.

Does reducing prices when a new firm tries to enter a market amount to an infringement of Article 86 or of Chapter II? Before it has incurred sunk costs in becoming established the new entrant may be more easily deterred than later. Where sunk costs are large in relation to variable cost, a reputation for dropping prices just when a new entrant appears may deter entry for many years, as potential entrants are unlikely to incur significant sunk costs if the incumbents are entitled to reduce their prices to their average variable cost. A new entrant may never be able to recoup such an investment.

On the other hand, competition in secret discounts may be the only form of price competition possible in concentrated markets. It is very important not to chill price competition for fear of fines or penalties nor to discourage the initial investment that enabled a firm to become dominant. Even a dominant firm should not be required to hold an umbrella over new entrants. For these reasons, the US courts have been very hesitant to extend the concept of illegal predation.

In *Oscar Bronner GmbH & Co. KG* v. *Mediaprint Zeitungs- und Zeitschriftenverlag GmbH & Co. KG and others*,[23] Advocate General Jacobs, when dealing with access to facilities claimed to be essential said that:

> "it is important not to lose sight of the fact that the primary purpose of Article 86 is to prevent distortions of competition—and in particular to safeguard the interests of consumers—rather than to protect the position of particular competitors. . . ."

It is consumers and not the new entrant that are protected by Article 86 as under US law.

---

[22] Draft of 30 July 1998, based on the Bill print dated 25 June 1998, after the Committee stage in the House of Commons, OFT 237, para. 5.17.

[23] Case C–7/97, Opinion of 28 May 1998, para. 58. The ECJ confirmed the results of its Advocate General, but did not articulate any theoretical analysis, judgment, 27.11.98.

Community Case Law

In *Compagnie Maritime Belge,*[24] the CFI confirmed a decision of the Commission treating the shipowners who met in the committees of a shipping conference as being jointly dominant over shipping services for the routes it covered. When a newcomer, G & C, started to compete on the routes, the members of the conference adopted various kinds of exclusionary conduct. Most of their joint conduct enjoyed the benefit of the group exemption from Article 85 for liner shipping, so could not be controlled under that Article.

Acting through the committees of the conference, the shipowners granted discounts to shippers who used only conference ships, and they tried to persuade the Zaïrean authorities to refuse permission to G & C to sail on the routes to and from Zaïre. Condemnation of such practices did not extend the existing practice of the Commission and I shall ignore them.[25]

The shipowners also organised a system of fighting ships. They arranged for the freight of whichever conference sailing left at a date closest to a sailing by G & C, to be reduced at their collective expense to the level charged by G & C and, on one occasion, below it. It was not alleged that these prices were below any level of cost, but selective price cutting was condemned by the Commission.

In *AKZO,*[26] the Court established that sales by a dominant firm below average variable cost must infringe Article 86 because they would be commercially sensible only if the dominant firm were able to exclude the victim of its predation and raise prices thereafter.[27] The ECJ added that in the context of a scheme to exclude a competitor, sales below even average total cost would be abusive (paragraph 72).

These cost-based rules would prevent a dominant firm from excluding a competitor that was more efficient that it was, but would not hold an umbrella over a less efficient competitor.

---

[24] Joined Cases T–24, 26 & 28/93 *Compagnie Maritime Belge Transports SA* v. *Commission* [1997] 4 CMLR 273, [1997] 1 CEC 74, appeal from *CEWAL*. On appeal C–395/96P.

[25] The ECJ has not confirmed that co-ordinating with a foreign government agency to exclude a competitor amounts to the abuse of a dominant position. There may be a constitutional right to lobby the government agency that controls a firm's activities abroad.

[26] Case 62/86 *AKZO Chemie BV* v. *Commission* [1991] ECR I–3359, [1993] 5 CMLR 215, [1993] 2 CEC 115, para. 71.

[27] The expectation of recoupment is treated by all economists as an important element of predation. The initial low prices favour consumers and lead to more of the product being produced. It is only if prices can be raised again after deterring the new entrant that consumers suffer. In Case C–333/94P *Tetra Pak International SA* v. *EC Commission* [1996] ECR I–5951, [1997] 4 CMLR 662, [1997] CEC 186, the ECJ confirmed that it was not for the Commission to prove an ability to recoup. It is thought that, at most, this altered the onus of proof. It may be that the Court considered that the case was so strong that there was no need for the Commission to establish a likelihood of recoupment.

The abuse, found by the Commission and confirmed by the CFI in *Compagnie Maritime Belge*, was meeting competition by reducing prices just when and where a new entrant appeared. The list of abuses of a dominant position is not closed. Selective price cutting may be an addition to predation condemned in *AKZO*. There are various possible explanations of the judgment which is currently before the ECJ.[28]

Collective Price Cuts

It may be that the Commission and Court were affected by the collective nature of the price reduction. A single firm must be allowed to meet competition or it may lose market share to a less efficient firm. Moreover, a rule removing the right to meet competition would reduce the incentive to invest in creating a new market. There is no reason why several incumbents should be allowed to collude to exclude a newcomer. Many people disapprove of the block exemption for liner shipping, which they say permits cartels, although others think that it is only through cooperation that regular sailings involving many vessels can be arranged.[29]

In any event, there is no language in the judgment to support the view that the CFI condemned only collective exclusion. Almost certainly the judgment applies to selective price cuts by a single firm or by jointly dominant firms.

Unilateral Selective Price Cuts

A more likely conclusion is that the Court considered that picking off new entrants to exclude by price cuts is abusive: competition can be met only by price reductions across the board and not by selective price cuts.[30] This prevents the incumbent from excluding even a less efficient competitor at low cost and has given rise to great concern.

On the other hand, an incumbent who has already invested a great deal of capital may have extremely low marginal or average variable costs. A newcomer that would have to face a reduction in prices to that level could

---

[28] The hearing has been held and Fennelly AG gave his opinion on 29 Oct. 1998. There are many more issues than I have mentioned, so judgment is not likely until well into 1999.

[29] For the history of fighting ships organised by conferences and for a discussion of aspects of the judgment I have ignored, see J. Tillotson and A. MacCulloch, "E.C. Competition Rules, Collective Dominance and Maritime Transport" (1997) 21 *World Competition—Law and Economics Review*, Sept. 51. Their article analyses acutely all the aspects of the decision and judgment in *Compagnie Maritime Belge*.

[30] In *Irish Sugar*, [1997] OJ L258/1, [1997] 5 CMLR 666, [1997] CEC2380, para. 129, the Commission condemned selective discounts made to buyers near the border, who might have bought their sugar from Northern Ireland. This may not be entirely relevant to meeting competition domestically, but tied up with market integration policy, which will not be relevant under Chap. II of the Bill. The Commission did, however, refer also to "applying different conditions to equivalent transactions".

never justify the investment needed to enter the market. If it expected to charge no more than the incumbent's average variable cost, entry might be deterred indefinitely if we had only cost-based rules.

Where a market is regulated by law, the incumbent is usually very dominant, having been the sole authorised supplier in the past. It is difficult for a regulator to supervise prices. How can he tell what level prices would have reached had there been more competition? Moreover, price regulation distorts investment decisions. A regulator may find it helpful to preserve even less efficient suppliers, as they may constrain the dominant firm somewhat. They may also become more efficient as they start operations and expand. A regulator might care to restrain a very powerful incumbent from reducing prices below a certain level. Deciding the best level requires, however, a great deal of information. He could announce in advance the formula he would use. as is being done by the Department of Transportation in the USA,[31] and in the USA and EC in telecommunications.

In the USA, and EC, suppliers of telephone services are being required to allow access to the local network to third parties. Both countries seem to be moving towards an access charge being allowed based on long run incremental costs. In the EC the incumbents are allowed to charge a little extra.[32] Charging a sum below the long run incremental cost may be treated as predatory.[33]

Calculation of long run incremental costs involves considerable discretion. The basis is the unit cost that the incumbent would incur if it were to increase the capacity of the network. Such calculations will not be based on actual costs. The concept is forward-looking and someone will have to try to imagine what they will be without being able to go out to tender for the various inputs. Different honest calculators may come to very different amounts. It is not a good test for courts to apply. It is far more appropriate

---

[31] The Department of Transportation in the USA was concerned that the price of seats on flights to or from the hub of an airline were some 40% higher than others of similar length. Only one new entrant had survived since deregulation 20 years ago. The Department alleged that when a new entrant appeared with a "no frills" service at low prices, the incumbent would reduce its prices and increase its flights at the same time as the newcomer's on the incumbent's and the newcomer's other routes. The Department proposed a formula that would constrain incumbents from reducing prices further than would make commercial sense in the short term. The proposal appeared on the internet: http://www.dot.gov/affairs.dkt3713.htm.

[32] See the Commission Recommendation of 8 Jan. 1998 on interconnection in a liberalised telecommunications market (Part I - Interconnection Pricing, [1998] OJ L73/42, recitals 3 and 5 and Art 3. When technology is continuously improving and reducing cost, a charge based on long run incremental cost will never allow the incumbent to recover its historic cost, so some top up is required to encourage investment.

[33] See J. Temple Lang, "European Community Antitrust Law: Innovation Markets and High Technology Industries", chap. 23 in Barry Hawk (ed.), [1996] *Fordham Corporate Law Institute* 519, 575, n. 117. Temple Lang is the director in charge of telecommunications within DGIV.

to regulators who can be consulted in advance by the incumbent, which employs a team of economists. When this or some other test is applied by a regulator, it is not as likely to be as confiscatory as when applied *ex post* by a court or competition authority under Article 86 or Chapter II.

Conclusion

While we are waiting for the judgment in *Compagnie Maritime Belge*,[34] it is difficult to know what the EC rule about meeting competition is, and therefore to apply clause 60 of the UK Bill. I have hopes that Advocate General Fennelly, who is an economist as well as a distinguished lawyer, may analyse the problems well before the UK Bill is passed. It might be helpful if the OFT were to indicate somewhat more precisely what is meant by predation. The draft guidelines condemn it but do not indicate what conduct is embraced by the term. Nor do they indicate awareness of the tension between incentives to invest initially to develop a new market and driving out competition by competition otherwise than on the merits.

In my view any limit to the permissible amount of a price reduction such as that proposed by the US Department of Transportation for airlines should be imposed by a regulator who can be consulted in advance by the incumbent. Not only would the regulator know a great deal more about the industry, and be served by economists, he could publish formulae in advance and change them if they became inappropriate. He would be available for consultation by the dominant firm.

I fear that selective price cuts by dominant firms may be treated as abusive under EC law, save in so far as roughly justified by cost savings to the incumbent.[35] It is most unfortunate that discrimination should be listed in Article 86 as an example of an abuse. It is silly to make illegal the only kind of price competition possible in concentrated markets. Economists welcome price discrimination in many, although not all, circumstances. It may suffice to meet a charge of predation to show that conditions are different.

Excessive pricing

There are many other questions that are likely arise under Chapter II. Article 86 specifically refers to unfair pricing as an abuse. Since *United Brands*[36] and *General Motors Continental NV* v. *Commission*,[37] the

---

[34] See n. 28 above.   [35] See *Irish Sugar*, n. 31 above, para. 150.
[36] 76/353/EEC, 17 Dec.1975 [1976] OJ L95/1, [1976] 1 CMLR D28, CMR 9800. On appeal, Case 27/76 *United Brands Co. and United Brands Continental BV* v. *Commission* [1978] ECR 207, [1978] 1 CMLR 429, CMR 8429.
[37] Case 26/75 [1975] ECR 1367, [1976] 1 CMLR 95, CMR 8320.

Commission has not challenged excessive pricing, because it does not know how to tell what would be a fair price. The ECJ referred to the economic value of the product in the cases cited, but in the *SACEM* cases,[38] it suggested comparing prices abroad. The problem is that prices abroad tend to be different because conditions are different, especially, especially when trade between member states is not appreciably affected.

Consequently, the Commission tries to avoid making such decisions, and leaves the matter to national authorities, as it did in the *Sacem* cases.[39] The OFT may, therefore, expect the Commission to leave such cases to it or to national courts to decide under UK law. The OFT guideline on Chapter II infringements at 5.11 states:

> "In general, the DG expects to follow the European Commission and be cautious in finding excess prices, in themselves, to be an abuse. He will be mindful of the need not to interfere in natural market mechanisms where high prices will encourage new entry and thereby serve to increase competition. Excessive prices are likely to be regarded as an abuse on in markets where an undertaking is so dominant, and new entry so unlikely, that the undertaking is in a position similar to a natural monopoly and it is clear that high profits will not stimulate successful new entry."

Where there is such strong market power, the industry may well be regulated, and regulators are in a far better position to set prices *ex ante* according to an announced formula. This is far more satisfactory than for the OFT or court to decide *ex post* that prices charged in the past are abusive. A regulator can be consulted in case of dispute.

Access to Essential Facilities

There are serious disadvantages to granting access to essential facilities.[40] First, the possibility of being required to grant access may discourage investment in the original facility. Secondly, it may discourage the duplication of a facility and, thirdly, it leads down the slippery slope to regulation. The first objection is less serious when the initial investment was made in the public sector, where financial incentives are less important.

---

[38] Case 110/88 *Lucazeau* v. *SACEM* [1989] ECR 2811, [1991] 4 CMLR 248, [1990] 2 CEC 856.

[39] *E.g.*, Case T–114/92 *Bureau Européen des Médias de l'Industrie Musicale* v. *Commission* [1995] ECR II 147, [1996] 5 CMLR 305, [1995] 1 CEC 592. The ECJ ruled on the criteria, the Commission prepared a chart of charges in different Member States, and the French Conseil de la Concurrence found that the prices were excessive. This enabled the French courts to deal with the matter.

[40] See A. Overd and W. Bishop, "Essential Facilities: the Rising Tide" [1998] ECLR 183 and D. Ridyard, "Essential Facilities and the Obligation to Supply Competitors under UK and EC Competition Law" [1996] ECLR 438.

If access is granted easily, many small firms may demand access so a substantial case law may be expected. The OFT guidelines at 5.33–5.34 provide virtually no analysis.

The Commission has gone very far in treating ports and airports as essential facilities, and finding that the incumbent enjoys a dominant position over narrowly defined markets. *Magill*[41] the judgment of the ECJ gave cause to great concern. The three television broadcaster whose programmes could be received in Ireland and Northern Ireland, each published a weekly guide to its own programmes but sued successfully for copyright infringement when Magill produced a comprehensive guide. There was fear that the holder of an important patent which had followed a very large investment in R&D would have to give a compulsory licence to an improvement licensee if there was demand for the improvement, as it would be a new product.[42]

Fortunately, the courts' case law has been far more restrained. The CFI confirmed in *Tiercé Ladbroke v. Commission*,[43] that there was no duty for

---

[41] *Magill* v. *TV Guide (Re the): ITP, BBC and RTE* v. *Commission* (89/205/EEC), 21 Dec. 1988, [1989] OJ L78/43, [1989] 4 CMLR 757, [1989] 1 CEC 2223; on appeal, Joined Cases T–69, 70 & 76/89 *Radio Telefis Eireann and Others* v. *Commission* [1991] ECR II–485 *et seq.*, [1991] 4 CMLR 586 *et seq.*, [1991] 2 CEC 114, 147 & 174 (CFI); Joined Cases C–241 & 242/91P *Radio Telefis Eireann and Others* v. *Commission* [1995] ECR I–743, [1995] 4 CMLR 718, [1995] 1 CEC 400 (ECJ).

[42] At the start of technical development, it may not be clear how wide a patent may be. In the USA, some have been very wide indeed. Barton refers to one for all transgenic rice. An exclusive right over a polypeptide chain may confer a monopoly not only on cures, but also testing kits. The former would probably not be possible in Europe, but the polypeptide chain for a virus has given trouble in Europe both at the opposition stage before grant and in the courts thereafter.

If the basic patentee can prevent exploitation by the holder of an improvement patent, there is insufficient incentive for the optimal amount of investment in improvement. See Professors Barton, Gallini and Trebilcock in a round table on the interface between competition and intellectual property to be published shortly by the OECD and placed on the internet. Should compulsory licences be required under the competition rules, or should such power be granted to the patent office even after grant. It is in a better position to understand the technology.

It might be more effective to narrow the scope of the basic patent when granted, but often patent examiners do not, at that time, understand the width of the exclusive right. There is no obvious solution.

To prevent obstacles to free movement the EC has, however, been adopting directives that raise national copyright to the highest level in any Member State, because that is easier to defend in the WTO. Are authors really induced to invest more effort because their great grandchildren will enjoy copyright for a further 20 years after the author has been dead for 50? It is more effective to limit the extensions to intellectual property made by harmonising directives to what is reasonably necessary to induce investment in protected products than to invoke the uncertain concept of essential facilities save in exceptional circumstances.

See http://www.oecd.org/daf/ccp/SERIES.HTM

[43] Case T–504/93, [1997] ECR II–923 [1997] 5 CMLR 309. There are several cases of *Ladbroke* v. *Commission*. It is important to check the Court's file number. I have criticised the reasoning relating to the relevant market: "The Ladbroke Saga" [1998] ECLR 169 but I am delighted that *Magill* has been construed narrowly. The judgment was an appeal from

the copyright holders of live film of French horse races to license Ladbroke in Belgium to show the films in its betting shops.

The reasoning for not applying *Magill* was weak and based on the surprising view that the films were ancillary to the supply of betting services and the definition of the market as that including films of all horse racing, not only French races. The CFI did not consider that the product was new, although I would have thought that the chance for the punters to see live films of the races was more novel and important than the comprehensive TV guide in *Magill*. The reasoning may have been unsatisfactory but it does show a determination by the Commission and CFI not to construe *Magill* widely.

We are still awaiting the judgment of the ECJ, in *Oscar Bronner GmbH & Co. KG v. Mediaprint Seitungs- und Zeitschriftenverlag GmbH & Co. KG and others*, followed the opinion of Francis Jacobs[44] in result, but did not articulate any theory. The Advocate General was clear and analytical. Mediaprint, a large publisher of newspapers in Austria, had built up the only nation wide home delivery service. Bronner was a small publisher. It claimed that Mediaprint's delivery service was an essential facility to which it claimed a right of access. This was an extreme case, even assuming that Mediaprint was dominant over newspaper delivery services.

The Advocate General, after considering *Magill*, *Tiercé Ladbroke* and earlier cases, summarised the US case law. He pointed out that there a monopoly supplier has a duty to supply only when five conditions are met.

1. the facility must be essential,
2. it must not be practical to duplicate it,
3. access on reasonable terms is denied to a competitor,
4. it is feasible for the facility to be provided, and
5. there is no legitimate technical or commercial reason for refusing access.

After saying (paragraph 58) that Article 86 is intended to protect consumers rather than competitors, he observed that the owner of the facility must have power in the market downstream. He also observed at the end of his opinion, at paragraphs 64–9, that granting access to essential facilities would require detailed regulation to fix the terms on which access was required.

At paragraph 63, he described the circumstances in *Magill* as being "very special". First, the existing television guides, each confined to a single broadcaster, were inadequate when compared with the position in

---

the Commission's unpublished decision to close the file, so not as satisfactory as an appeal against a decision on the substance. The judgment has been appealed, Case C–300/97P. The Commission published its decision to close the file in *PMI/DSV* [1995] OJ L221/34, [1996] 5 CMLR 320, a similar decision stating that there was no obligation to grant a licence in Germany, where an exclusive one had already been granted to DSV.

[44] Case C–7/97, Opinion of 28 May 1998.

other countries, so the exercise of the copyright to restrain Magill from publishing a comprehensive guide prevented a much needed new product from coming to the market. Secondly, the copyright in information was hard to justify in terms of rewarding or providing an incentive for creative effort.[45] Thirdly, since the useful life of the programmes is short, the exercise of the copyright would create a permanent barrier to entry.

Access could be required only in return for compensation for the risk as well as the investment costs. Such intervention in the market would be justified only when the owner of the facility had a stranglehold on the related market. It must be extremely difficult for others to compete without access to the facility. Bronner might not be able to duplicate the national home delivery service, but there were numerous alternative methods of distribution.

The ECJ followed the results of the opinion, and in my view this strengthens the theory articulated by Mr Jacobs. This will do a great deal to chill claims to access to facilities. I am delighted, as the need to grant access must reduce the incentive to the original investment in the facility. It is so easy for a smaller firm to claim that the market would be more competitive if it had access to a facility that has already been built. The reduction in the incentive to invest in the original facility and in its duplication seems less pressing when the investment has been made in an individual case. Moreover, courts and national authorities would find great difficulty in setting terms for a contract that the supplier does not want to make.

Where the incumbent built up the facility at the expense of the taxpayer, I am less concerned by the essential facilities cases, and the doctrine has been most widely used in transport cases, where this was the case. Incentives to investment may be less important to public undertakings than to private, and after privatisation are often controlled by a regulator, who would have less trouble in setting terms.

Telecommunications incumbents have huge advantages in using their local networks. Until microwave systems and access through cable television networks undermine this monopoly, access to the local network really is necessary to a telecommunications company. It would not be practical to duplicate it. However, when there is a dispute as to the charge for interconnection, the regulator can decide it *ex ante*,[46] which is a great deal more satisfactory than for a court or competition authority.

---

[45] This is hard to reconcile with the view expressed by the ECJ in *Magill* that in the present state of Community law, before harmonisation, it is for national law to determine the extent of intellectual property rights. I am delighted that Mr. Jacobs was prepared to make the point in open court. It has been made by several commentators and must have affected the gut reactions of the judges.

[46] See text around n. 32 above.

Conclusion

The ECJ habitually forbids as abusive exclusionary practices by a dominant firm unless they amount to competition on the basis of performance. It has never stated what this means. It is tempting to refer to efficiency, as has been done in the USA since about 1980. Until this step is taken, it is difficult to guess what practices may be condemned by the Community Courts and, therefore, difficult to predict the position under UK law by reference to clause 60.

Many experts have been delighted by the opinion of Advocate General Jacobs in *Oscar Bronner* which limits the number of cases demanding access to essential facilities that might have swamped the courts and OFT. The draft guidelines by the OFT do not adequately stress the tension between the advantages of making competition in the related market stronger, and the reduction of the incentive to the original investment in sunk costs which may have been risky.

6

Regulation under the Competition Act and Existing Legislation for the Regulation of Utilities

JOHN SWIFT QC*

Introduction

This Chapter covers four issues:

(i) the purpose and likely effect of the Competition Act generally;
(ii) the likely impact of the new Competition Act on the utilities;
(iii) the future regulatory framework for the utilities: substantive rules and conditions;
(iv) the future regulatory framework for the utilities: procedural rules and safeguards.

The Purpose and Likely Effect of the Competition Act Generally

In its manifesto for the May 1997 election, the government promised more effective and more accountable regulation. Admittedly that promise was made in respect of public transport and, in particular, railways, but the principles of greater effectiveness and accountability apply to the Competition Act as they apply to the regulation of utilities.

Greater effectiveness means that the prohibitions of anti-competitive conduct and abuse of dominant position should be expected to effect changes in behaviour. An Act of Parliament directed to improving the competitiveness of the national economy has a most important purpose: clear signals to commercial undertakings that workable and effective competition is an objective and a requirement of the State. It is not a discretionary matter for those undertakings. Agreements which have an appreciable effect on competition require justification by reference to settled criteria; otherwise they are void. Conduct of a dominant firm which

---

* Rail Regulator, Office of the Rail Regulator, at the time of writing.

seriously and unjustifiably distorts competition is similarly prohibited. And the State expects that regulators will make the legislation effective. Thus the task of regulators in pursuing those political and economic objectives is (i) to clarify the rules of behaviour which are not compatible with the proper functioning of competitive markets or acceptable behaviour by dominant firms and (ii) to use the powers at their disposal to detect and stop prohibited conduct and require and enforce changes which are fair and reasonable.

Greater accountability is much more than the introduction of a right of appeal to the Competition Commission. Each of the regulators is, in my view, accountable for the vigorous and independent exercise of powers to improve the competitiveness of the markets in question, subject to any overriding political, social or financial considerations which are seen by the State as having greater priority; and the effectiveness of regulatory performance should ultimately be judged by the efficiency with which those markets operate.

Thus greater effectiveness and accountability cannot be achieved without a rule based system in which the appropriate economic and legal principles apply. Which system to adopt usually involves difficult choices. And the United Kingdom has deliberated for a long time on the merits of a prohibition-based system of law. But a system based on established and developing principles of EU law—both substantive and procedural—has plain advantages.

Community law has been part of our *corpus juris* since accession in 1973: not just in the area of competition law but more generally. The twinned principles of supremacy and direct effect have already been applied in this country for 25 years, with profound and lasting consequences for the rights and duties of undertakings and for the protection of individuals. It is also eminently sensible, in my view, for the government to have incorporated the principles of Articles 85 *and* 86 because the two are inextricably linked and serve the same economic objectives. Moreover the concepts of legal certainty, of the right to be heard, of due process generally, are not alien to our democracy. On the contrary, I believe there is a growing demand for transparency and for consistency which can only be met by the development of rules of procedure after consultation processes, and their objective and non-discriminatory application. This has even greater force when the penalties for infringement can be so severe.

The Competition Act, therefore, has political and economic objectives supported by a framework of rules for the application of the appropriate principles of law. I now turn to the impact of the new Act on the utilities.

The Likely Impact of the Competition Act on the Utilities

Common Characteristics of the Utility Markets

The five sector-specific statutes[1] governing the establishment and regulation of the utilities also have political and economic objectives, in their case set out in the opening sections of the legislation, reflecting the importance to the economy of the utilities and the need for effective regulation.

In my consideration of this subject therefore I group together the supply of gas, electricity, water, telecommunications and railway services. Though each market[2] has distinctly individual characteristics they share two common and, for the purposes of the new Competition Act, significant features.

First, within each utility market there is at least one company occupying a position of dominance satisfying the test laid down in *United Brands* v *Commission*[3]:

> "a position of economic strength enjoyed by an undertaking which enables it to prevent effective competition being maintained on the relevant market by affording it the power to behave to an appreciable extent independently of its competitors, customers and ultimately of its consumers."

Secondly, in comparison with the structure of the markets at the time of privatisation, each of the utility markets has since been liberalised to a greater or lesser degree. Generally competition has been introduced into all product markets other than those occupied by a single "natural monopoly" dominant firm so that choice between suppliers can be exercised by consumers and users and greater value for money achieved.

Application of Chapters I and II Prohibitions

Chapter II

The first of these common features, the existence of one or more dominant undertakings, means that the Chapter II prohibition will be of considerable relevance and importance in the utilities markets. Any abuse affecting trade within the United Kingdom committed by the utility service provider which is in a dominant position will cause that service provider to be in breach of the Chapter II prohibition.

The dominant utility undertaking will be subject to a system of law which is of direct and immediate effect. Any breach will render that under-

---

[1] Telecommunications Act 1984, Gas Act 1986 (and 1995), Electricity Act 1989, Water Industry Act 1991 and Railways Act 1993.

[2] I am assuming for the purposes of this chap. that separate "relevant product markets" are likely to exist within the more general description of a "utility" market.

[3] Case 27/76 [1978] ECR 207, [1978] 1 CMLR 429.

taking liable to a fine by a regulator and probably also to third party enforcement actions[4] irrespective of a prior finding of breach or an order made by statutory instrument.

But if the "sector specific" legislation is already effective in controlling exploitative and anti-competitive abuse by dominant firms, is the Chapter II prohibition going to be used? Does it require from the dominant firm a change in behaviour from that allowed under the utility's licence to operate the relevant "regulated" assets?

In my view the Chapter II prohibition is relevant in each of the utility markets, irrespective of whether the conditions in the regulated company's licence are fit for purpose. The prohibition, in effect, incorporates into English law those principles which apply generally to all dominant firms and which derive from a system of judge made law (interpretation and application of the Treaty) rather than a set of conditions for the grant of a right to operate a regulated business. In many respects the licence conditions seek to put into the form of specific obligations the kind of conduct which would be the opposite of an abuse, but they lack adherence to a set of general principles of law.

Equally it would, in my view, be quite wrong to assume that unless conduct is expressly prohibited by the licence it cannot amount in law to an abuse. Licences provide substantial protection for licensees from arbitrary behaviour by regulators. They constitute their "rights" at a time when they assumed sectoral responsibilities for the provision, for example, of universal services. Thus they can only be changed by agreement or after review by the MMC concluding, in effect, that without amendment the licence operates against the public interest.

But the origin of these rights and duties lies in an executive decision by Government or regulator. That plainly does not exclude the prohibition of Chapter II, to the extent that the conditions in the licence fall short of the rules of conduct demanded by the application of Community principles.

Chapter I

The second common feature, the liberalisation of the markets, means that regulation gradually shifts emphasis from straightforward issues of the pricing and performance of the dominant firm—the exploitative type of abuse—to issues of anti-competitive conduct, whether engaged in by the dominant firms (Chapter II) or by the new entrants (Chapter I). As the markets are liberalised, new opportunities for competition between suppliers will present themselves—there will be increased scope for competition between incumbents in the same industry (for example, in the water and sewerage industries), between undertakings which initially were

---

[4] See Kon and Maxwell, "Enforcement in National Courts of the EC and new UK Competition Rules: Obstacles to Effective Enforcement"[1998] E.C.L.R. at 443 and the authors' reference to *Hansard Pepper* v. *Hart* statements. See also s. 60(6)(b) of the Act.

service providers in different sectors (witness the interest shown by electricity undertakers in the gas industry and vice versa) and, of course, competition between incumbents and other new entrants. Resistance by an undertaking to compete, whether through agreement between undertakings or, if dominant within the sector, by unilateral refusal to supply, will be subject to a prohibition and the sanctions that flow from its breach.

Thus the utility undertakings and other businesses in their markets will be subject to common rules and have a right to expect uniformity and consistency in their application. For the utilities this is a significant development. The utilities are currently regulated by legislation specific to each utility sector and according to objectives which differ between sectors. This is a major change and one which promotes the Community principle of legal certainty. It requires full analysis by business, its advisers and regulators to ensure that existing and future conduct is compatible with the Community principles.

Future Regulatory Framework: Substantive Rules and Conditions

The Competition Act is undoubtedly a significant development in UK competition law although the system of law incorporated into it is familiar.

(i) Many businesses, including the utilities, whether UK or foreign-owned, already have experience of the principles of European competition law as defendants, complainants or interested observers. These businesses have, at least since the United Kingdom joined the European Community, been subject to the direct effect of the competition prohibitions of the Treaty of Rome, including being beneficiaries of block and individual exemptions. They have already been influenced by the prohibitions, Council Directives and Commission Notices. They will be aware of the powers of the Commission, of the readiness to use heavy fines to secure compliance and of the processes available to secure proof of violation. Indeed, referring to the prohibitions in Articles 85 and 86 of the Treaty of Rome, the Government Minister, Lord Simon of Highbury, said[5]:

> "In my previous life I dealt with [the prohibitions] for 20 years. I did not find much difficulty in understanding them because I believe that most businessmen understand what an abuse is."

(ii) The developments in competition policy in European competition law and American anti-trust law have influenced the decisions of the

---

[5] Lord Simon of Highbury, House of Lords – Report Stage, 23 Feb. 1998, *Hansard* col. 516 .

competition authorities in the United Kingdom, principally the MMC, but also decisions taken by the Director General of Fair Trading under the Competition Act.

(iii) These concepts have also influenced the regulatory regime to which the utilities are subject. For example, the Railways Act 1993 recognises the concept of a right of access on reasonable terms to an essential facility (infrastructure, stations and light maintenance depots), regarding the occupier of the essential facility as a dominant firm and controlling refusal to supply or discrimination or both. In terms of legal certainty, the same Act requires the Regulator to exercise his functions so as to enable railway companies to plan for their future with a reasonable degree of assurance.

(iv) The concepts can also be found in several of the licences granted to utilities or amended after agreement: see for example the Fair Trading Condition contained in BT's licence. Another is the Exclusionary Behaviour Condition contained in the licences of Passenger and Non-Passenger Train Operators. This condition enables the regulator to prevent behaviour by a licence holder who is in a dominant position if the regulator considers such behaviour may unfairly exclude or limit competition in the supply of railway services. The government was clearly influenced by the prohibition in Article 86, now reflected in the Chapter II Prohibition.

I argued above that effective utility regulation under sector-specific legislation and licence does not exclude the broader Community principles. Equally, I see no reason why the licence conditions should become redundant merely because of the application of more general principles. Licence conditions represent, in effect, undertakings given by a utility to secure the performance of statutory duties: in sufficient detail to provide "legal security" and effective monitoring while allowing sufficient flexibility to avoid excessive intrusion by the regulator. Again, using a railways example, Railtrack's licence was amended in 1997 so as to impose a new obligation on Railtrack to secure the maintenance, renewal and replacement and improvement, enhancement and development of the network so as to satisfy the reasonable requirements of operators and funders. The reason for the amendment was to increase Railtrack's accountability as a dominant firm.

But the licence conditions of utilities are not simply those conditions which control exploitative or anti-competitive abuse. They also reflect the unique importance of utilities in our society. The United Kingdom has gone further in the EU in the speed and comprehensive restructuring of its utilities from publicly-owned and publicly-controlled monopolies to privatised companies, linked to each other by regulated contracts and licences. But the concept of an obligation to provide a universal service is central to utility regulation.

Indeed it is a critically important "accountability" of a regulator to secure that the utility can provide such a service: from BT's village callboxes to Railtrack's infrastructure. These public-interest obligations already form part of the substantive rules of behaviour for utilities, reflecting the views of Parliament, and will continue. They are sector-specific and derive their validity from the purposes of the legislation. They do not necessarily fall within the more general type of "abusive" behaviour defined by the Court under Article 86.

Thus because of the importance attached to the utility services, I believe that the utility undertakings will continue to be regulated using sector specific tools, at least until the services can be guaranteed to be provided in a fully contestable market. In the railways industry, for example, safety, insurance and claims handling will continue to be regulated as public service obligations.

Future Regulatory Framework: Due Process and Rights of Undertakings

Increased transparency, predictability and consistency is already demanded by undertakings and by government in respect of utility regulation. The Competition Act will reinforce those demands.

Primary Role for Sector Regulators

As is predominantly the current case, competition functions will generally be exercised by the relevant sector regulators as opposed to the Director General of Fair Trading in respect of any matter to be considered in his sector. This avoids the need for duplication of expertise and ensures that undertakings within a sector are treated on a fair and consistent basis. However, consistency of approach across markets is also important and will be achieved through the new mechanisms, in particular, the role of the Concurrency Working Group and the guidance to be provided by the regulators.

The Importance of the Guidance under Sections 51 and 52

Guidance will be provided by the Director General of Fair Trading and the sector regulators having concurrent powers. The guidance will explain the application of the Chapter I and II prohibitions and how the regulators intend to enforce the prohibitions. The draft guidelines published to date concern the general principles applicable to all businesses. They may not be sufficient for undertakings operating in the utility markets and there may be a need for sector-specific guidelines to be prepared to supplement the general guidance. The guidelines are prepared after consultation with the other regulators with common interest.

The Concurrency Working Group

Representatives from the offices of each of the sector regulators are members of the Concurrency Working Group chaired by a member of staff from the Office of Fair Trading. The Group will provide the forum for the sharing of information about cases and the development of policy. Information about complaints and notifications received and investigations in progress or contemplated will be shared between the various regulatory offices. This will include, where appropriate, the sharing of information about cases being considered using the sector specific powers: for example, an investigation of an alleged breach of licence condition. The establishment of the forum is an important development. With the exception of the obligation requiring the sector regulator to consult the Director General of Fair Trading (and vice versa) before exercising competition functions, any cross-office discussion occurring at present is on an *ad hoc* and voluntary basis.

Publication and Transparency

Procedural rules prepared by the Director General of Fair Trading after consultation with the sector regulators and approved by the Secretary of State for Trade will be published. These will provide transparency and certainty, regarding process matters to businesses who are under investigation or who have notified agreements or conduct to the Director General of Fair Trading. All the regulators will, when exercising their functions, continue to meet their obligations to act according to the rules of natural justice.

Appeals Process

The new regime also introduces an appeals process, the use of which will provide clarity and assist in ensuring consistency. Undertakings which are the subject of a decision of the Director General of Fair Trading or a sector regulator will be able to appeal against or in respect of that decision. There is provision also for third party appeals. Appeals will be decided by the newly created appeal tribunal with the ability for appeals to be made to the

Courts of Appeal or Session on points of law arising from a decision of the appeal tribunal or in respect of the decision of the appeal tribunal as to the amount of penalty payable.

Regulatory Discretion as to Use of Powers

Where there is overlap, the regulators will have choice whether to use the enforcement powers contained in the sector specific legislation or the new competition powers. They will also, after having commenced an investigation, be able to change from one regime to the other. This is sensible. Lord Simon of Highbury[6] explained the policy as follows:

> "We consider that the regulator should not be committed, once and for all, to taking action only under the provisions of the Bill. If circumstances change, or indeed his assessment of the situation changes, he has to retain the ability to take action to enforce the licence condition. A breach of a licence condition cannot be allowed to continue just because a regulator has started to take action under the prohibitions and then found, for whatever reason, that was not an effective route for dealing with the breach."

Conclusion

Undertakings carrying on business in the utility markets account for about 10 per cent of GDP. Those markets are characterised by the existence of dominant firms, increased liberalisation and social and environmental concerns. Their performance and competitiveness are critical to the UK economy and its ability to compete in worldwide markets.

In the period from 1984 to 1993 (from the Telecommunications Act to the Railways Act), the United Kingdom adopted a system of regulatory controls which were "sector specific": that is to say that the content of the licences required by the operators of the regulated assets depended upon the purposes sought by Parliament at the time of legislation. But they *did* incorporate concepts similar to those found in the principles of Community law; they *were* based on mandatory obligations "to do or not to do" certain things; in some cases fines could be levied for licence breach; and powers *were* conferred on regulators to obtain information.

Thus in the utility sector the United Kingdom was already practising in a branch of Community competition law—and developing the concept of abuse as dominant firms found themselves subject to competition from new entrants.

The Competition Act will not displace the licence conditions so long as

---

[6] Lord Simon of Highbury, n. 5 above, col. 495.

they remain (a) the kind of specific obligations required to comply with the Chapters I and II prohibitions and (b) of a type which must be present to meet the political and social objectives which formed the justification for privatisation: essentially "market failure" conditions where required outputs would not ordinarily be expected from the operation of market forces.

Subject to that, the Competition Act introduces new duties and new rights for utilities, in their capacity as dominant firms. It also empowers and, in my view, requires sector-specific regulators to adopt an approach towards competition and the rooting out of indefensible anti-competitive agreements which is vigorous and supports the intentions of Parliament.

It is too early to predict the proportion of regulatory decision-making which will be "Competition Act" as distinct from "sector-specific" legislation. But it must be expected that in classic Chapter II areas of abuse, certainly in the case of new decisions by dominant firms, the processes of enforcement by the regulator and appeals for the dominant firm would tend to make the Competition Act the preferred route for both. That would also promote the goal of uniform systems of regulation backed by uniform and statutorily required processes.

It is a major challenge and opportunity for all involved, undertakings, advisers and regulators.

7

UK and EC Competition Laws: Will They Operate in Complete Harmony?

AIDAN ROBERTSON

Introduction

The Competition Act is designed to rationalise the application of competition law in the UK, in particular by ensuring that the UK regime operates as harmoniously as possible with the EU regime. In this chapter, I intend to examine whether substantive harmony is likely to reign. I do not intend to address the separate question of whether procedural harmony is also likely to occur, an issue that arises out of the interaction of competition courts and authorities at EU and national level.

The Competition Act is designed to rationalise the application of UK competition law to restrictive trading agreements by repealing the Restrictive Trade Practices Act 1976 ("RTPA") and replacing it with a prohibition on anti-competitive agreements modelled on the prohibition imposed by Article 85 of the Treaty of Rome.

The RTPA has long been a minefield for lawyers, being both a trap for the unwary and difficult to navigate even for those who seek to comply. Danckwerts LJ's observation in *British Basic Slag*[1] that aspects of the legislation are "calculated to drive any accurately minded lawyer to despair" is no less true today.

In the first part of this chapter, I will explain the structure of the Act, then consider the prohibitions in detail and then identify the principal ways in which those prohibitions depart from EC competition law. In the second part, I will set out the ways in which it is sought to avoid UK law diverging unnecessarily from EC law.

The Act is divided into four parts:

Part I - Competition
Part II - Investigations in relation to Articles 85 and 86

---

[1] (1963) LR 4 RP 116 at 149.

Part III - Monopolies
Part IV - Supplemental and Transitional.

There are also 14 Schedules:

1. Exclusions: Mergers and Concentrations;
2. Exclusions: Other Competition Scrutiny;
3. General Exclusions;
4. Professional Rules;
5. Notification under Chapter I: Procedure;
6. Notification under Chapter II: Procedure;
7. The Competition Commission;
8. Appeals;
9. Director's Rules;
10. Regulators;
11. Interpretation of section 55 (disclosure of information);
12. Minor and Consequential Amendments;
13. Transitional Provisions and Savings;
14. Repeals and Revocations.

Part I of the Act is divided into five Chapters. The main purpose of Part I is to create new prohibitions based upon Articles 85 and 86 (or Articles 81 and 82, as they will be under the consolidated EC Treaty following ratification of the Treaty of Amsterdam[2]). These will be called respectively the Chapter I and Chapter II prohibitions. These will work in similar ways to Articles 85 and 86, with the possibility of exemption under the Chapter I prohibition, including block exemption. An EC exemption will have automatic effect as a parallel exemption under the UK legislation. There will be *de minimis* exceptions to the Chapter I and Chapter II prohibitions, though the rules setting these out have yet to be drafted (as is the case with the other subordinate legislation under the Act, including the block exemptions). The government has indicated that these will be turnover based and the appropriate level of turnover will be in the region of £20–50 million.[3]

Under Chapter III, the Director General of Fair Trading ("DGFT") is going to play the role of the European Commission under the Act, though with enhanced powers of investigation and enforcement. The DGFT will be able to fine businesses breaching the prohibitions up to 10 per cent of their annual turnover. However, under Chapter IV, unlike the European Commission, there will be an appeal by way of rehearing before an appeal tribunal of the Competition Commission (as the revamped Monopolies and Mergers Commission is to be renamed), thence appeal with leave on a point of law to the Court of Appeal.

---

[2] Now not expected until Spring 1999.
[3] H L Hansard, 17 Nov. 1997, col. 434.

Under Chapter V, sectoral regulators (water, gas, electricity, rail and telecoms) will also be able to exercise the DGFT's powers concurrently with the DGFT. Indeed, OFTEL already operates similar powers under the Fair Trading Condition it first introduced into BT's operating licence[4] and which now applies in most telecoms licences.[5]

The Chapter I Prohibition

Chapter I is divided into 16 sections. Section 1 repeals the RTPA along with the Resale Prices Act 1976, the Restrictive Practices Court Act 1976 and the Restrictive Trade Practices Act 1977. Sections 2–16 thus set out the Chapter I prohibition. Section 2 imposes the basic prohibition. It provides:

"(1) Subject to section 3 [excluded agreements], agreements between undertakings, decisions by associations of undertakings or concerted practices which—

(a) may affect trade within the United Kingdom, and
(b) have as their object or effect the prevention, restriction or distortion of competition within the United Kingdom,

are prohibited unless they are exempt in accordance with the provisions of this Part.

(2) Subsection (1) applies, in particular, to agreements, decisions or practices which—

(a) directly or indirectly fix purchase or selling prices or any other trading conditions;
(b) limit or control production, markets, technical development or investment;
(c) share markets or sources of supply;
(d) apply dissimilar conditions to equivalent transactions with other trading parties, thereby placing them at a competitive disadvantage;
(e) make the conclusion of contracts subject to acceptance by the other parties of supplementary obligations which, by their nature or according to commercial usage, have no connection with the subject of such contracts.

(3) Subsection (1) applies only if the agreement, decision or practice is, or is intended to be, implemented in the United Kingdom.

(4) Any agreement or decision which is prohibited by subsection (1) is void.

(5) A provision of this Part which is expressed to apply to, or in relation to, an agreement is to be read as applying equally to, or in relation to, a decision by

---

[4] A challenge to which by way of judicial review was rejected by the Div. Ct.: *R. v. OFTEL, ex parte BT*, unreported, 20 Dec. 1996 (Phillips LJ and Hooper J).
[5] See OFTEL Press Release 5/98, 3 Feb. 1998.

an association of undertakings or a concerted practice (but with any necessary modifications).

(6) Subsection (5) does not apply where the context otherwise requires.

(7) In this section 'the United Kingdom' means, in relation to an agreement which operates or is intended to operate only in a part of the United Kingdom, that part.

(8) The prohibition imposed by subsection (1) is referred to in this Act as 'the Chapter I prohibition'."

The Chapter I prohibition largely faithfully follows Article 85(1) and (2). It differs:

(i) by not having a requirement of an effect on inter-EU trade, and by providing that the prohibition may apply to an agreement which only affects trade within a part of the UK and which has the object or effect of distorting competition within only a part of the UK. There is seemingly no *de minimis* threshold to assessing what constitutes a "part" of the UK.[6]

(ii) by not applying to agreements excluded under section 3.

Otherwise the Act applies to all agreements and concerted practices, as well as to decisions by trade associations. This means that all horizontal agreements, save those involving full merger, are subject to the Act, such as joint ventures, R&D agreements or other types of co-operation. While a trade association as such will not be caught by the Chapter I prohibition, the agreement to set it up might be and any decisions, including recommendations, that it makes will be caught, just as they currently are under EC law.

Vertical agreements are, for the present, also to be caught, unless the Secretary of State exercises the power of exclusion under section 50(1). For the time being, it appears that all types of distribution agreements will require scrutiny. However, the definition of what constitutes an agreement still poses problems under Article 85, and hence the Chapter I prohibition, in the context of unilateral decisions implemented through a distribution network.[7]

Excluded Agreements

Section 3(1) provides that the Chapter I prohibition does not apply to agreements excluded by Schedules 1–4 of the Act. There is no equivalent provision in Article 85(1), although the Merger Control Regulation does,

---

[6] Contrast the merger control provisions under the Fair Trading Act 1973 which require an effect on competition within at least a substantial part of the UK: see *R. v. MMC, ex parte South Yorkshire Transport* [1993] 1 WLR 23.

[7] See *Adalat* [1996] OJ L201/1 and Case T–41/96 *Bayer v. Commission* [1996] ECR II-383 discussed below.

in effect, withdraw agreements forming part of a concentration from scrutiny under Articles 85 or 86.

Schedule 1, which may be amended by the Secretary of State under section 3(2), excludes agreements entered into as part of mergers (including newspaper mergers) which fall to be considered under the Fair Trading Act 1973 or concentrations over which the European Commission has exclusive jurisdiction under the Merger Control Regulation.

Schedule 2 excludes agreements which fall to be scrutinised under competition provisions in other legislation, principally the Financial Services Act 1986, the Companies Act 1989, the Broadcasting Act 1990 and the Environment Act 1995. Rather than adopt a similar approach to professional rules (as was originally envisaged), Schedule 4 simply enables the Secretary of State to designate professional rules as falling within the exclusion. The professions concerned are listed in the Schedule.

Schedule 3 is wide-ranging and potentially far-reaching. Following the paragraphs of the Schedule, it excludes agreements which:

(1) implement planning obligations under the Town and Country Planning Act 1990;
(2) the Secretary of State had directed not to be referred to the Restrictive Practices Court under section 21(2) RTPA, unless the DGFT directs otherwise;
(3) relate to the constitution, rules or guidance of an EEA regulated securities market;
(4) is entered into by an undertaking to enable it to carry out a duty either of providing services of general economic interest or being a revenue-producing monopoly. This provision, tucked away in this Schedule, is equivalent to Article 90(2) EC, and is likely to be of great significance;
(5) is required to comply with a legal requirement;
(6) is excluded by the Secretary of State to enable the UK to comply with its international obligations;
(7) is excluded by the Secretary of State for exceptional and compelling reasons of public policy;
(8) relates to a coal or steel product over which the European Commission has exclusive jurisdiction;[8]
(9) relates to production or trade in an agricultural product and forms part of a national market organisation, is necessary to attain the objectives of Article 39 EC or is a non-price fixing agricultural cooperative.

---

[8] This will lapse if the coal and steel fall back within the scope of the EC Treaty on the expiry of the ECSC Treaty.

The DTI is still considering whether to add to these categories of excluded agreement by excluding, pursuant to section 50, vertical agreements and/or agreements relating to the use of land.

Individual Exemption

Section 4 sets out the DGFT's power to grant individual exemption for agreements from the Chapter I prohibition if meeting the criteria for exemption set out in section 9 (which mirror those in Article 85(3)). Agreements requiring exemption must be notified under section 14. Under section 5, the DGFT may cancel or vary an exemption if he believes there to be a material change in circumstances or he reasonably believes that he was misled in granting exemption.

Block Exemption

Section 6 sets out the DGFT's power to issue block exemptions for categories of agreement likely to meet the criteria for exemption under section 9, section 7 permits the use of an opposition procedure in such block exemptions and section 8 sets out the procedure under which such a block exemption may be made.

Parallel EC Exemptions

Agreements which have been individually exempted by the European Commission or which are block exempt (including those which have benefited from exemption under the opposition procedure) are also exempt from the Chapter I prohibition under section 10. This parallel exemption extends to agreements which would be block exempt were it not for lack of effect on inter-State trade. However, the Director may vary or cancel the parallel exemption (though not, of course, the EC exemption), subject to any argument that an EC exemption precludes stricter national measures.[9]

Article 88 EC Exemptions

Section 11 permits the Secretary of State to grant an exemption from the Chapter I prohibition to give effect to a ruling under Article 88 EC. At

[9] See Case C–70/93 *BMW* v. *ALD* [1995] ECR I–3439 and Case T–266/93 *Bundeskartellamt* v. *Volkswagen* [1995] ECR I–3477 in which Tesauro AG delivered an Opinion that national law could not impose stricter controls on agreements exempted under block exemptions.

present, the principal importance of this provision is in relation to international air alliances.[10]

Procedure

Individual exemption may be obtained by way of an application under section 14. Notification precludes the DGFT fining the parties to the agreement for the period from notification to the date of determination of the application for a decision. Under section 16, a decision that the agreement does not infringe the Chapter I prohibition is binding on the DGFT unless he has reasonable grounds to believe that there has been a material change of circumstance since his decision or he reasonably suspects that he was misled.

As an alternative to notification for exemption, an agreement may be notified under section 13 for guidance whether the agreement is likely to infringe the Chapter I prohibition. While this guidance will not have the legal effect of an exemption, under section 15 it will protect the parties from further proceedings by the DGFT if he takes the view that the agreement does not infringe, unless and until the DGFT has reasonable grounds to believe that there has been a material change of circumstance since his decision or he reasonably suspects that he was misled.

Enforcement

Enforcement of the prohibitions is dealt with under Chapter III. Infringement of the Chapter I prohibition entitles the DGFT to investigate the parties to the agreement (sections 25–31) and to direct an infringing agreement to be varied or terminated (section 32). Directions under section 32 are enforceable through court action under section 34, and the DGFT may also adopt interim measures under section 35 pending completion of an investigation in order to prevent serious, irreparable damage to a person or to protect the public interest.

Under section 36, the Director may impose a penalty on a party to an infringing agreement of up to 10 per cent of that party's annual turnover, unless the agreement falls within the category of "small agreements" established under section 39. Small agreements are non-price fixing agreements where the parties have a small combined turnover and/or a small market share. It would appear that the DTI intends to define this category by reference to turnover alone, as is currently done under the Restrictive Trade Practices (Non-notifiable Agreements) (Turnover Threshold) Order 1996,[11]

---

[10] See the EC Competition Law (Articles 88 and 89) Enforcement Regulations 1996, SI 1996/2199.

[11] SI 1996 No 348.

that threshold currently being set at £50 million.[12] Small agreements thus
have limited immunity from fines unless and until the DGFT removes that
immunity under section 39(4); the other consequences of infringement,
particularly voidness of restrictions under section 2(4), nevertheless remain.

The Act is silent about the possibility of private rights of action for
breaches of the Chapter I prohibition. The government's view is that the
right to sue for damages and/or an injunction under the Act is to be equivalent to that which would be available under Articles 85 and 86.[13] Hence
section 60(6)(b) specifically provides that the UK courts are to be guided by
the European Court and Commission in deciding whether damages should
be available.

Chapter II Prohibition

The Chapter II prohibition is, at least on its face, a good deal simpler than
the Chapter I prohibition, because—as with EC law—there is no exemption from an abuse. There are, however, excluded categories of conduct
which escape the prohibition.

Section 18(1) provides that:

> "Subject to section 19 [excluded categories], any conduct on the part of
> one or more undertakings which amounts to the abuse of a dominant
> position in a market is prohibited if it may affect trade within the United
> Kingdom."

Section 18(2) repeats the list of prohibited conduct to be found in Article
86. Section 18(3) makes it clear that a dominant position is to be assessed
in the UK or in any part of the UK, and section 18(4) dubs this prohibition
"the Chapter II prohibition".

Section 19 excludes conduct excluded under Schedule 1 or 3 (see above).

Conduct may be notified for guidance under section 21 or a decision that
it does not infringe the Chapter II prohibition under section 22 (but not
exemption). Similar provisions apply as those discussed above.

Harmonious Interpretation: The Consistency Principle

A key feature of the Act is the consistency principle which seeks to achieve
the objective of harmony of interpretation. Under the consistency
principle, UK law should not diverge in its substantive application from EC

---

[12] SI 1997 No 2944.
[13] Hansard, 25 Nov. 1997, col. 956: Lord Haskell: "[t]hird party rights of action are to be
the same as those under Articles 85 and 86".

law. Businesses are or should be already well used to the need to comply with EC competition law. UK law should not apply different or more rigorous standards under its competition law than those under the Treaty of Rome. Therefore, a business complying with EC competition law should be able to continue its agreements and practices without the need to change or even review them to comply with the new UK law.

The Act will arise for judicial interpretation in two principal ways:

(a) in appeals from the Director General of Fair Trading ("DGFT") and Competition Commission;
(b) in normal civil or criminal litigation.

Under section 49 issues of interpretation of the Act will first fall to be determined at Court of Appeal level and then, with leave, the House of Lords.

However, the prohibitions in the Act will be able to be pleaded by parties in civil or criminal litigation in any court or tribunal with the necessary jurisdiction. So competition defences may be pleaded in actions based upon contract, tort or restitution, as well as in direct breach of statutory duty claims under the Act (assuming the Act does in fact permit such an action). Similarly, the Act may be relied upon should the legality of an agreement or practice arise in criminal proceedings.

However the issues arise and whatever the court, the judiciary will be faced with the interpretation of an Act based upon what are likely to be unfamiliar principles of EC and economic law. How much and what guidance may the judiciary rely upon under the Act?

Section 60(1) of the Act declares that its purpose is:

"to ensure that so far as is possible (having regard to any relevant differences between the provisions concerned), questions arising under this Part in relation to competition within the United Kingdom are dealt with in a manner which is consistent with the treatment of corresponding questions arising in Community law in relation to competition within the Community."

Section 60 then provides that:

"(2) At any time when the court determines a question arising under this Part, it must act (so far as is compatible with the provisions of this Part and whether or not it would otherwise be required to do so) with a view to securing that there is no inconsistency between—

(a) the principles applied, and decision reached, by the court in determining that question; and
(b) the principles laid down by the Treaty and the European Court, and any relevant decision of that Court, as applicable at that time in determining any corresponding question arising in Community law.

(3) The court must, in addition, have regard to any relevant decision or statement of the Commission.

(4) Subsections (2) and (3) also apply to—

    (a) the Director; and
    (b) any person acting on behalf of the Director, in connection with any
        matter arising under this Part.

(5) In subsections (2) and (3), "court" means any court or tribunal.
(6) In subsections 2(b) and (3), decision includes a decision as to—

    (a) the interpretation of any provision of Community law;
    (b) the civil liability of an undertaking for harm caused by its infringe-
        ment of Community law."

Seemingly a simple provision, this does in fact raise some real problems of
interpretation. First, the general principle is one of consistency, except
where there is a relevant difference. Thus, if an exclusion were to be introduced for vertical agreements, it is clear that the principle of consistent
interpretation is overridden to the extent necessary to give effect to that
exclusion.

However, there are other differences in drafting in the Act where it is
unclear whether the difference is intended to be relevant. The Chapter II
prohibition, apparently intended to be a mirror of Article 86, prohibits in
section 18(1) "any conduct on the part of one or more undertakings which
amounts to the abuse of a dominant position" whereas Article 86 simply
prohibits "any abuse by one or more undertakings of a dominant
position". It is unclear whether the term "conduct" is intended to restrict
the ambit of the Chapter II prohibition to sins of commission, not
omission. Would a refusal to supply constitute "conduct" for the purposes
of section 18(1)?

The consistency principle is declared to apply "in relation to competition". It is thus not apparent on the face of the Act whether it extends to
procedural issues arising out of the DGFT's powers of investigation and
enforcement under the Act, and whether it excludes general principles of
EC law (such as proportionality, non-discrimination and fundamental
rights) which are equally applicable in the competition sphere. But, the
government minister responsible for the Bill in the Lords, Lord Simon of
Highbury, confirmed in Committee stage that general principles of
Community law are to be imported into the Act under this section.[14] This
does not, however, mean that the DGFT's procedural rules have to be
modelled on those under which the European Commission operates.

Nor should it be assumed that simple application of the consistency
principle will be sufficient to solve problems of interpretation. The ambit
of some of the most basic concepts of competition law is not free from
doubt and uncertainty. For example, section 18(1) referred to above refers
to the concept of an abuse of a dominant position by one or more undertakings: so-called joint, collective or oligopolistic dominance. This is a

---

[14] Hansard, 25 Nov. 1997, col. 962.

concept which the European Court has almost studiously refused to define except in the most general terms.

Most recently, in *Compagnie Maritime Belge* v. *Commission*[15] the Court of First Instance upheld the Commission's decisions that three liner conferences infringed Article 85 and that the participants had infringed Article 86. The Court came very close to ruling in paragraph 64 of its judgment that parallel conduct is caught by Article 86:

> "As a result of the close relations which shipping companies maintain with each other within a liner conference, they are capable of implementing in common on the relevant market practices such as to constitute unilateral conduct. Such conduct may involve infringement of Article 86."

The development of EC law in this way is, in part or in whole, explicable by the lack of investigative powers into industries characterised by parallel conduct. Since the UK is to retain the complex monopoly provisions in the Fair Trading Act 1973, such a wide definition is arguably unnecessary.

Similarly in relation to the Chapter I prohibition on anti-competitive agreements, the definition of what constitutes an agreement still poses problems under Article 85 in the context of unilateral decisions implemented through a distribution network.

In *ADALAT*[16] the Commission condemned Bayer for breaching Article 85 by refusing to supply pharmaceutical wholesalers who were engaged in parallel trade of those drugs. The President of the Court of First Instance suspended the Commission's decision requiring Bayer to continue supplying wholesalers. The President noted that the Commission's decision raised "the particularly delicate question as to the circumstances in which a refusal to sell is capable, when it occurs in the context of continuing commercial relations, of constituting one of the aspects of an agreement containing an export prohibition" and that it did not appear "at first sight" that there was sufficient consent by the wholesalers to Bayer's refusal to supply to create an agreement capable of being caught by Article 85.[17]

Can these problems be resolved by referring a question of interpretation under Article 177 of the EC Treaty[18]? Article 177 provides:

[15] Joined Cases T–24–26 & 28/93 *Compagnie Maritime Belge* v. *Commission* [1996] ECR II–1201, on appeal to ECJ as Case C–395/96P. Fennelly AG's Opinion was delivered on 29 Oct. 1998.

[16] [1996] OJ L 201/1.

[17] Case T–41/96 *Bayer* v. *Commission* [1996] ECR II–383, paras. 41–52. EC law is not alone in finding unilateral conduct difficult to categorise (although the English courts have taken a robust approach to this question: see *Cound* v. *BMW* [1997] EuLR 277 and *Clover Leaf Cars* v. *BMW* [1997] EuLR 535). The US Court of Appeals for the Tenth Circuit has only recently decided that tying practices by a supplier when carried out contrary to the wishes of a purchaser are nevertheless subject to the prohibition on anti-competitive agreements under s. 1 of the Sherman Act 1890: *Systemcare Inc.* v. *Wang Laboratories Inc.* [1997] ECLR R–152.

"The Court of Justice shall have jurisdiction to give preliminary rulings concerning:

(a) the interpretation of this Treaty;"

Since the Competition Act is a domestic UK statute it does not obviously fall within the jurisdiction of the Court of Justice to give a ruling on its interpretation. In *Kleinwort Benson*[19] the Court of Justice rejected a request from the Court of Appeal for a preliminary ruling under an equivalent procedure in the Brussels Convention on Jurisdiction and Judgments on the basis that the English law in question, the Civil Jurisdiction and Judgments Act 1982, although clearly modelled on the Brussels Convention, was in fact purely domestic, concerning at it did the allocation of jurisdiction between the English and Scots courts. The Court has, however, since held that it does have the jurisdiction to rule on national law in appropirate circumstances.[20]

The position was most recently set out in the Court's judgment in *Bernd Giloy* v. *Hauptzollamt Frankfurt am Main-Ost*[21]:

"[20] According to settled case-law, the procedure provided for in Article 177 of the Treaty is a means of cooperation between the Court of Justice and national courts. It follows that it is for the national courts alone which are seised of the case and are responsible for the judgment to be delivered to determine, in view of the special features of each case, both the need for a preliminary ruling in order to enable them to give their judgment and the relevance of the questions which they put to the Court (see, in particular, the judgments in *Dzodzi*, cited above, paragraphs 33 and 34, and in Case C–231/89 *Gmurzynska-Bscher* [1990] ECR I–4003, paragraphs 18 and 19).

[21] Consequently, where questions submitted by national courts concern the interpretation of a provision of Community law, the Court is, in principle, obliged to give a ruling (see *Dzodzi* and *Gmurzynska-Bscher*, cited above, paragraphs 35 and 20 respectively). Neither the wording of Article 177 nor the aim of the procedure established by that article indicates that the Treaty makers intended to exclude from the jurisdiction of the Court requests for a preliminary ruling on a Community provision where the domestic law of a Member State refers to that Community provision in order to determine the rules applicable to a situation which is purely internal to that State (see *Dzodzi* and *Gmurzynska-Bscher*, cited above, paragraphs 36 and 25 respectively).

[22] A reference by a national court can be rejected only if it appears that the procedure laid down by Article 177 of the Treaty has been misused and a ruling

---

[18] The government takes the view that a reference may be made under Art. 177: see Lord Simon, HL Hansard, 25 Nov. 1997, column 963.

[19] Case C–346/93 *Kleinwort Benson* v. *City of Glasgow District Council* [1995] ECR I–615.

[20] Joined Cases C–297/88 and C–197/89 *Dzodzi* v. *Belgium* [1990] ECR I–3763; Case C–231/89 *Gmurzynska-Bscher* v. *Oberfinanzdirektion Köln* [1990] ECR I–4003.

[21] Case C–130/95 *Bernd Giloy* v. *Hauptzollamt Frankfurt am Main-Ost* [1997] ECR I–4291.

from the Court elicited by means of a contrived dispute, or it is obvious that Community law cannot apply, either directly or indirectly, to the circumstances of the case referred to the Court (see, to this effect, *Dzodzi* and *Gmurzynska-Bscher*, cited above, paragraphs 40 and 23)."

A further question is whether the DGFT and the Competition Commission constitute a court or tribunal from which a reference may be made under Article 177; the case law of the European Court indicates that only the latter is a tribunal capable of utilising the Article 177 procedure.[22]

As well as being guided by the European Court, the UK courts are required "in addition, [to] have regard to any relevant decision or statement of the Commission". Interestingly, nothing is said about having regard to anything emanating from other European institutions. Therefore, there is no express scope for looking at legislative intent, for example in minutes of meetings of the Council of Ministers or in debates in the European Parliament. On the other hand, the UK courts will be able to look at the Commission's Competition Decisions, *Annual Competition Policy Reports*, Bulletins, letters on behalf of the Commission and even Commission Press Releases as an aid to interpretation.

Further, the Commission being an executive body and separate from the European Court is not an authoritative source of EC law, although its pronouncements may be regarded as being of persuasive value. In many areas of EC competition law, there is a dearth of even complete absence of Court case law, leaving the UK Court reliant on the Commission statements.

In practice, the Commission's interpretation of EC law is quite capable of diverging from that of the European Court, sometimes quite significantly. For example, in the *Schöller*[23] and *Langnese-Iglo*[24] cases, the Court of First Instance held that the Commission had quite simply wrongly interpreted and applied the law on the application of Article 85 to exclusive purchasing agreements. And in other cases, the Commission may simply interpret EC law in a way which goes beyond that which the Court has hitherto adopted. The concept of joint or collective dominance under Article 86, referred to above, has been used by the Commission in cases of purely parallel conduct, particularly in relation to cases under the Merger Control Regulation, whereas the Court, so far as it has developed the concept, requires there to be some underlying economic link between the dominant undertakings.

Moreover, the Commission's views change over time. The present consultation over its policy on vertical restraints is an illustration of this.

---

[22] But see Case C–54/96 *Dorch Consult* v. *Bundesbaugesellschaft Berlin* [1997] ECR I–4961, and the Opinion of Leger AG in Case C–44/96 *Mannesmann* v. *Strohal Rotationsdruck* [1998] ECR I–73.

[23] Case T–9/93 *Schöller* v. *Commission* [1995] ECR II–1611, not appealed.

[24] Case T–7/93 *Langnese-Iglo* v. *Commission* [1995] ECR II–1533: appeal dismissed, Case C–279/95P, judgment of 1 Oct. 1998.

But sometimes the Commission's published announcements fail to keep pace with modern Commission thinking. The present Notice on exclusive dealing contracts with commercial agents[25] dates from 1962, but it would be dangerous to place reliance upon it as representing the Commission's present views on the application of Article 85 to agency agreements.

This is not to say that UK courts should not have regard to the European Commission. However, there is a danger that by an over-rigid application of section 60(3), UK courts will place too much reliance upon statements by the Commission, and will be precluded from having regard to other aids to interpretation to be found in other sources.

There is also a danger that the UK courts will become blinkered by the consistency principle in their approach to interpretation, and will not take into account the wealth of common law competition law authority to be found on the other side of the Atlantic. US antitrust, the second oldest competition legislation in the world, is relevant to many of the questions which arise before the European courts. Various Advocates General have referred to US authority; for example, Roemer AG in the seminal case of *Consten & Grundig*[26] said that:

> "American law (the "*White Motor Case*") requires for situations of the type before us a comprehensive examination of their economic repercussions. Clearly I do not mean to say that we should imitate in all respects the principles of American procedure in the field of cartels. This would not in fact be justified by reason of the essential differences between the systems . . . But such a reference is useful nevertheless in so far as it shows that in respect of Article 85(1) also it is not possible to dispense with observing the market *in concreto*. It seems to me wrong to have regard to such observation only for the application of paragraph (3) of Article 85."

Advocate General Roemer proved to be at least a quarter of a century ahead of his time, as the Court did not follow this advice at the time, and has only recently begun to do so.

Further, other national laws within Europe have influenced the development of EC competition law, notably German law, and continue to do so. There seems to me no good reason why judicial decisions on the application of such laws should not be taken into account, if relevant. Indeed, nowadays, as there are over 50 national competition law regimes,[27] there is a great wealth of competition law authority available for the UK courts to draw upon. While it is clearly desirable that the UK courts should not depart from EC law without good reason, it would be wrong for section 60 to prevent the UK courts from having regard to other laws where relevant, since those laws may be taken into account by the European Court in

[25] [1962] JO 2921.

[26] Joined Cases 56 & 58/64 *Consten & Grundig* v. *Commission* [1966] ECR 299, 358.

[27] Figure quoted by M. Bloom, "International Co-operation between Competition Authorities", *Lawyers' Europe*, Autumn 1997, 3.

developing Community competition law.

The danger of being blinkered by the consistency principle illustrates a danger of subsidiarity: that it becomes a one-way street. In other words, while EC law may influence the development of UK competition law, the converse will be prevented from happening. This would in my view be unfortunate. National law has a role to play in examining and shaping concepts of Community law, just in the same way as US federal circuit courts do with federal law, subject always to the ultimate control of the Supreme Court. Provided that a national court may be subject to the overall guidance of the Court of Justice under the Article 177 procedure (see *Bernd Giloy*, discussed above), it seems to me that creative tension between the UK and European courts should be viewed as a constructive, not destructive, force for the development of a more rational competition law.[28]

Conclusion

This second part of my chapter has considered the relatively narrow, if fundamental, question of judicial interpretation in ensuring procedural harmony. The question is narrow, because interpreting the law is only the first step in its application. UK courts have little experience of applying economic law. The soon to be defunct Restrictive Practices Court did decide a considerable number of cases under the Restrictive Trade Practices Act 1976, principally in the late 1950s and early 1960s, in which it was required to apply economic law, and despite being a specialist tribunal, almost all its most important decisions granting exemption to cartels have been subject to cogent and convincing criticism.[29] In my view, interpretation of the new Act will raise fewer problems than its application in practice.

---

[28] For a discussion of the relationship between federal and state antitrust in the USA, see Hawk and Veltrop, "Dual Antitrust Enforcement in the United States: Positive or Negative Lessons for the European Community" in Slot and McDonnell (eds.) *Procedure and Enforcement in EC and US Competition Law* (1993), (Sweet & Maxwell, London).

[29] Stevens and Yamey, *The Restrictive Practices Court: A Study of Judicial Process and Economic Policy* (Weidenfeld and Nicholson, London, 1965).

Index